The Pr

Preaching with Imagination

Cyril S Rodd

Other titles in the series

1 *Why Preach?*, Peter Dawson
2 *Preaching on the Old Testament*, Christine Pilkington
3 *Variety in Preaching*, Brian Galliers
4 *Preaching in a Cultural Context*, Martyn D Atkins
5 *A Woman's Perspective on Preaching*, Jane V Craske
6 *Preaching as Doctrine*, John B Taylor

ISBN 1 85852 214 5

To my wife, who thinks (rightly) that
too many books are written, but who has
nevertheless always allowed me to add
to their number without complaining

Cyril S Rodd is a Methodist minister. He spent almost the whole of his ministry in teaching posts, first at Handsworth Methodist College, Birmingham, and then at Southlands College, later a constituent college of Roehampton Institute of Higher Education (now The University of Surrey, Roehampton). He was editor of *The Expository Times* for 25 years until his retirement in 2001.

GENERAL INTRODUCTION

Preaching is a very particular form of communication which has always been important in the life of the Christian Church. At the beginning of the twenty-first century we are undergoing a revolution in the varieties, method and speed of our communications. Preachers of all denominations, ordained and lay, undertake this calling with an awareness that we preach in a changing context.

The Preacher's Library is designed to help us to think through, perhaps in some cases reassess, why we preach, how we preach, and to whom we preach. Some of the volumes in this series will take a fresh look at familiar issues, such as how preachers should approach various parts of the Bible, how we understand and express our doctrinal inheritance and the variety of styles in which preaching can be done. Other volumes will introduce issues which may be less familiar to many of us, such as the significance of our cultural context or the way in which the self-understanding of a woman preacher has important things to say to all preachers. Some of these books will offer direct help in the practice of preaching. Others will deal with issues which, although they appear more theoretical, impinge upon the preacher's task and on which we therefore need to have reflected if we are to preach with integrity in today's world.

All the writers in this series, lay and ordained, women and men, are recognised preachers within their own denominations and write with the needs of their colleagues firmly in mind. These books will avoid academic jargon, but they will not avoid dealing with difficult issues. They are offered to other preachers in the belief that as we deepen our thinking and hone our skills God's people will be blessed and built up to the glory of God.

One of the most common criticisms of sermons is that they are dull and boring. As a member of the congregation once said to me about the previous Sunday's preacher: 'He told us everything he knew about Deborah.' The implication was clear: 'And he thought *that* was preaching!' We preachers need to stretch our imaginations so that we approach our subjects and our texts in ways that relate them to lived experience. Cyril Rodd's *Preaching with Imagination* will help us to do just that. Cyril is a church musician as well as a preacher, and hears a good many sermons from his place on the organ stool. Imagination is the quality he too often finds lacking in what he hears. In this zesty and enthusiastic book he explores ways in which we might remedy that deficiency. In the process he makes us think deeply about what preaching is as well as about how we do it. Reading this book could and should be a transforming experience.

Michael J Townsend

CONTENTS

'He's a poor gawk-hammer. Look at his sermon yesterday.'

'His sermon was well enough, a very good guessable sermon, only he couldn't put it into words and speak it. That's all was the matter wi' the sermon. He hadn't been able to get it past his pen.'

'Well – ay, the sermon might have been good; for, 'tis true, the sermon of Old Eccl'iastes himself lay in Eccl'iastes's ink-bottle afore he got it out.'

Mr Penny, being in the act of drawing the last stitch tight, could afford time to look up and throw in a word at this point.

'He's no spouter – that must be said, 'a b'lieve.'

''Tis a terrible muddle sometimes with the man, as far as spout do go,' said Spinks.

Thomas Hardy, *Under the Greenwood Tree*

1

IMAGINATION

Congregations are extraordinarily patient and generously courteous. Sometimes seated on the organ stool I look around the church during the sermon. All the faces are turned towards the preacher. They all seem to listen with close attention to every word that the preacher utters. It is very rare to see anyone yawn or fall asleep. As the congregation leaves after the service and they shake hands with the preacher, many of them, I am sure, thank him or her for 'the word', or for a 'beautiful service'. Yet as I listen to the sermon, my own reaction is often the same as it was many times when I watched a student giving a lesson in school. 'Why is this so utterly boring? What could be done to liven it up?' I used to tell my students that if they fail to be interesting, all is lost. The mounting noise in the class showed this very plainly. Fortunately for preachers rowdy behaviour by the congregation is not the penalty for dull sermons!

The aim of this little book is to encourage preachers to apply their imagination to the writing of the sermon. Sadly, imagination is often the least developed of all of our faculties. We exercise our bodies. We train our minds. We search out knowledge. We endeavour to find the truth. In preparation for making the sermon commentaries or one of the many books of notes or reflections on the Lectionary readings are carefully studied. The three readings are anxiously compared, even when the readings were not intended to be related. In all this imagination gets left behind. Yet for the preacher stirring up the imagination is the most vital of all the activities in the preparation of the sermon.

The vital imagination

We underrate imagination. Usually it is linked with the poet or musician. So it is. No poem was ever written, no symphony ever composed, without the imagination of the poet or the composer being energised. It is the imagination which makes the difference between doggerel and poetry. This is not to deny that a skilled musician ever writes pot-boilers. Because he or she has superb technique, even the pot-boilers may be attractive to listen to. The great works of art, however, are inspired by the imagination. It is the imagination which makes them vibrant and lifts them out of the ordinary and into the eternal.

But imagination is not limited to poets and musicians. All the great scientific discoveries have been made by men and women who allowed their imaginations to move beyond the accepted assumptions of their day. What is 'lateral thinking' but letting the imagination leap beyond conventional ideas to grasp fresh possibilities and novel ways of doing things? Of course, there has to be much dull, routine reading and learning before that leap is possible. Sir Alexander Fleming might have simply cursed when he noticed that something had killed off some of the bacteria in his specimen trays due to some carelessness. It was imagination which enabled him to see that what had happened might enable germs in the human body to be killed. In his autobiography, Sir Peter Medawar, whose researches into discovering how the body discriminates between its own and other living cells were massively important in making organ transplants possible, stresses the importance of imaginative speculation.[1] (He also points out that having a range of interests assists the effectiveness of the scientist, something which preachers might well take to heart.)

Imagination is probably the most important virtue that we can possess. It might seem surprising to call it a virtue. Think. How often are bad deeds done because the man or the woman who does them cannot *imagine* how the victim will feel, or what the full consequences of what they have done will be. How often do we fail in little acts of kindness because we have not *imagined* the hollowness there is in the heart of the person we might have helped and did not. How often do we disappoint a child through lack of imagination? Instead of giving them what they *really* want we provide something that we think is better. Or we push an urgent question aside because we are busy and tell them to ask later on, a 'later on' which never comes. And all because we could not *imagine* how they felt. Sympathy is 90 per cent *imagination*, for even if we have trod that way as well – the illness of a close relative, the death of a wife or husband, that dreaded diagnosis that took away all feeling and left us alone with dark despair – we are not that other person. The gap between us can be bridged only by imagination.

Robert Lynd tells us that everyone at every great hour of their lives – hours of passionate happiness or passionate sorrow – is aware of the futility of common speech. In the presence of love and death they are dumb. But not contentedly dumb. For they realise that while they possess the words that are adequate for the common objects of everyday life in the office or the shop, they need a deeper language to speak of sin and purity and holiness and God. They need the language of poetry, the language of imagination.

He goes on to claim that imagination is not a 'brilliant faculty of lying'. To scorn the imagination is to be a blind person deliberately refusing the miracle of sight. 'It is imagination that cleanses the scales from our eyes, and awakens our senses to the real things that surround us.' 'Where there is no imagination,' he warns us, 'there is cruelty, selfishness, death. ... When Christ announced that all men were his brothers, he taught us to look on other people imaginatively and not as though they were ciphers in a statistical abstract.'[2] Robert Lynd was writing in 1921. His words need to be heeded still more today, when it requires an imagination that is sensitive and alert to creep behind the league tables of schools and hospitals and the statistics of road casualties and redundancies to see each individual, who is just a number to the politicians and the administrators.

Robert Lynd's plea for poetry might equally be seen as a plea for imaginative preaching. What congregations are looking for is not exalted doctrine or urgent exhortation. They are looking for the beauty of holiness, that perception of the mystery and grandeur of God which they can find nowhere else but in our churches and through liturgy, scripture, hymn, sacrament – and preaching.

The imagination stifled

Imagination is desperately needed in sermons, yet so many things inhibit it.

In the first place, ministers and clergy (and even lay preachers) have to preach too often. Once a month would be plenty if imaginative sermons are to be written. Yet there is the treadmill of a sermon each Sunday – perhaps even two. This is aggravated by the Lectionary, unrelenting in its demands which make it impossible for preachers to take their sermons to other churches and so reduce the need for a new sermon each week. Sermons were always ephemeral, but if they can only be preached once (or kept in cold storage for three years!) there is less incentive to work at them and allow time for the imagination to play upon the text. Imagination requires time, but a busy life allows too little space to pause and allow the imagination an opportunity to become active.

Faced with the brief life of the sermon, the preacher has to be resolute. C S Lewis proposed a test for good writing: how often does it deserve to be read? The greatest novels rank high. Cheap magazine stories come at the bottom of the scale.[3] The message it gives to the preacher is dire. Preachers must not allow themselves to be corrupted by the fact that the life of a sermon is but 20 minutes. It may be that the sermon was good enough to be listened to more than once: the Lectionary forbids it, and congregations have a curious allergy to being offered 'secondhand' sermons. Even if it should pass C S Lewis's test, there is no opportunity to preach it again.

It must also be recognised that not every preacher every week finds his or her imagination immediately kindled by any of the three Bible readings, while some passages which they treasure and which might have awakened the imagination have been left out of the Lectionary. So the preacher has to work all the harder to create a sermon which enthuses him or her, and which, because of this, will excite the congregation.

Preachers also feel themselves under pressure to expound the readings of the Lectionary, and never take a poem or a novel as the basis for the probing of perennial human dilemmas – guilt and forgiveness, the entail of sin, the agony of suffering, goodness of character and the ambiguities of life. In this book I shall assume that the preacher normally takes the Lectionary readings (or one of them) as his or her 'text'. At the same time I have a slight regret that the tyranny of the Lectionary has killed off many other imaginative ways of presenting the Christian message or tracing out one or other of the deep issues of human living.

There is one further influence which stifles the imagination. In the past, and to a large extent still, the emphasis has been placed on obtaining a 'correct' understanding of the text. How often does the preacher feel the need to explain the background to the Old Testament reading? How often does the congregation have to trail wearily after the guide as he or she enlarges on the thought of St Paul or summarises attitudes towards the Samaritans in first-century Palestine? Perhaps recent new approaches to the Bible – reader-response criticism, rhetorical criticism and the like, which treat the Bible as literature rather than a doctrinal or historical deposit – may shift the preacher's emphasis. Even so, too many preachers seem to think that to provide an understanding of the reading is the main purpose of the sermon, which turns into an exegetical commentary, with its stress on the intellect and a pushing aside of the emotional and imaginative. Yet imagination is not hostile to the interpretation of the text or the reconstruction of the history. Indeed, my argument is that it is only the imagination which can lead to an appreciation of the text which will carry over to the congregation.

Enlightenment

For it is only the imagination which can lead to enlightenment. Many of us can recall moments when the voice of an actor or the interpretation of a pianist, or even the explanation of the teacher or lecturer, opened our eyes for the first time to unexpected beauties and meanings, which had previously been totally outside our experience. We had read and listened, but had never heard or been grasped by the splendour. Perhaps we may never experience the same exalted surprise in quite the same way again, but the memory remains, and has moulded part of our life. Robert Davidson, the former Old Testament Professor in the University of Glasgow, we are told, had the ability 'to see things from an unexpected angle, and through seeing to shed light in dark corners'.[4] That is what imagination does. That is what the preacher should aim at.

One last point: the sermon is part of worship. Even if the time has long gone when churchgoers used to refer to the 'preliminaries' and regarded the sermon as the high point of the service, the sermon is one of the main ways in which the congregation is helped to glorify God. The quality of the sermon, therefore, often determines the quality of the worship. An imaginative sermon will enable the hearers to draw close to God and offer him their praise, confession and thanksgiving. The tragedy is that so often the sermon is the low point in a service. The readings carry their own splendour. The liturgy, despite its limping modern language, still manages to retain something of the glory that Cranmer once gave it. The person offering the intercessions has worked hard to mould them into an offering worthy of God. It is at the moment when the preacher enters the pulpit (or stands to give an 'address' from the lectern or the chancel steps) the spirit of worship falters.

In what ways, then, can the imagination breathe life into the sermon, and how can preachers nourish their imagination so that their sermons can bring enlightenment to those who listen to them?

The way we shall travel

After a brief glance at the strange land of the Bible, I shall look at the text itself, suggesting five ways in which the imagination can be brought to bear on the readings. Since the sermon is spoken, a chapter will be devoted to the language preachers use, for nowhere is the imagination more needed than in selecting the right words and phrases in which to clothe their ideas. Then I shall consider how literature and music can help to awaken the preacher's own imagination and bring life into the sermon. Finally there will be a short discussion of beginnings and endings, before presenting three examples of the way imagination can invigorate a tired sermon.

2

ENTERING A STRANGE LAND

A foreign land

When we open the Bible we are entering a foreign land. We don't realise this, because the Bible (in the Authorised Version, or sometimes, further back, the Geneva Bible which Shakespeare knew) has become part of English literature. So true is this that, in these secular days, English departments in our universities are having to put on courses on the Bible so that their students can understand the poetry and novels that they will be reading, and editors of poetry and novels have to add footnotes explaining the biblical references, though often we discover they miss allusions that only those brought up on the English Bible are aware of. Yet many biblical phrases still remain in ordinary speech, even if the young think of suicide when they hear of 'the Samaritans'. Alister McGrath has collected over 20 such literal renderings of the Hebrew or Greek, some of them so much part of our normal speech that we hardly realise where they came from: 'to lick the dust', 'sour grapes' (but isn't that an amalgam, with part of the metal supplied by Aesop?), 'from time to time', 'the skin of my teeth', 'to put words in his mouth', 'the salt of the earth', 'the powers that be'. McGrath also lists some phrases which are minor variants of the AV originals, such as: 'rise and shine', 'fly in the ointment', 'a drop in the bucket'.[1] To these we might add 'mess of pottage', which trade unionists, if no one else, still trot out, although it has been almost entirely lost in our everyday speech.

It is little wonder, therefore, that many Christians assume that the Bible belongs completely to our world and speaks directly to us. Perhaps much of it does. But often it speaks to us because we have forced it to fit our own society and ways of thinking. We have not travelled to the strange land of the Bible as tourists and then stayed on as resident aliens. We need to remember Goethe's solemn warning:

Wer den Dichter will verstehen
Muss in Dichter's Lande gehen.

'Anyone who wants to understand a poet must go to the poet's country.'[2]

Psalm 23

The 23rd Psalm has comforted the dying, given hope to the bereaved, offered reassurance to the anxious, been a friend to the lonely, and brought strong support to those overwhelmed by the pressures and troubles of life. Its appeal and influence are immense. It lies beneath many of our hymns ('The God of love my Shepherd is', 'The King of love my Shepherd is', 'The Lord's my Shepherd, I'll not want', and verses in many others). It has been translated many times, in prose and poetry, from Wycliffe to the present. Modern paraphrases, such as 'The Lord is my Pilot, I shall not drift', 'The Lord is my Pace-setter, I shall not rush', 'My (mountain) Guide is the Lord: he will not let me wander', 'The Lord is like my Probation Officer', and the version of an 11 year old schoolgirl, 'The Lord is my Teacher', are both fascinating in their own right and offer imaginative ways of presenting the Psalm to congregations today.[3] But they do not take us back to the land of the psalmist.

As for the original Hebrew psalm, we have no idea who wrote it, or when. Was it sung by a king? Possibly. We do not know. We cannot even be sure of the images. Does the poet picture God first as shepherd and then as the host at a banquet? Or does he also introduce the idea of God as our guide? So the psalm which is so well known is really totally strange. It is its 'afterlife' that is familiar.

We may be fully satisfied with that afterlife. That is how most of us read it and most of our congregations understand it. The later descants drown out the original melody. Perhaps we only know the descant, as has happened with some well known tunes that were originally descants to melodies that have been forgotten. Yet there is the danger that what we hear is not a descant that genuinely grew out of the melody, but our own tune superimposed upon it and replacing it. We need to pack our bags and set out for that strange country and listen to the native airs.

(As an aside, I might observe that those of us within the churches, preachers in particular, are probably unaware of how much of the language we use in church is unable to climb out of the ghetto into which most people in our society have confined us. Dr D H C Read, one-time minister of Madison Avenue Presbyterian Church, New York, tells us that once he conducted a small wedding where few of the guests were connected with any church. During the service he read from 1 Corinthians 13 in a modern translation. The one question he was asked at the reception was, 'Who wrote that piece you read about love?' And when he told them, there was almost a gasp of disbelief – St Paul?[4] A minister told me once that to the lads in his inner-city area, 'crucified' belonged only to football. 'They crucified us' is the phrase they used when their local team was soundly beaten. What do those outside of the churches make of 'salvation' or 'atonement'? Imagination is needed here as well. But to return to our theme.)

One merit of the AV is that its language, archaic when it was first translated, makes it immediately obvious that it does not belong to our world. Modern translations, such as the *Good News Bible*, obscure this, and the Lectionary, by eliminating the more alien passages, makes its own contribution to this veiling.

Not as tourists

The Bible is a strange land. It is a land where only adult men counted, and where war was accepted as a matter of course and never seen as a problem. In that land there was never any suggestion that it was a religious duty to eliminate poverty, even though the rich had a duty to give charity to the poor and not use their power to oppress them. Animals were treated as superior tools, and the normal act of worship was to kill a sheep, a goat, or a bull (never any other species of animal), drain out its blood, dash the blood against the altar, and then cut up the animal, burning part of it on the altar and eating the rest as a social meal. In this strange land ritual purity was as important as morality, and honour often stood higher than ethics.

Tourists often fail to see what they are gawking at because they interpret it through their own experience. Listen to some of the comments made by members of a guided tour as you go round a church or castle. The same is true of tourists to that foreign land which is the Bible. We all interpret its words, stories and ideas by what is familiar to us through the experiences and feelings that we have imbibed from the spirit of our own age and the home and community in which we grew up. So we spiritualise the Sermon on the Mount (unless we have been seized by liberation theology, when we lock it into a political situation). We react against Abraham's treatment of Sarah, supposing that she would have felt as oppressed by the patriarchal society in which she lived as the most ardent feminists of today. We find it incomprehensible, grossly unjust, and morally wrong that Achan's sons and daughters should have been executed with him because he had taken some of the spoil from Jericho, for we live in an atomistically individualistic society. We interpret sacrifice in terms of the forgiveness of sins instead of the removal of uncleanness, which it often – perhaps usually – was. So to understand and sympathise with the men and women of the Bible we need to do more than travel to that strange land, taking our crisps and fish and chips with us. We need to join an Israelite family, worship with them, listen to the settling of lawsuits by the elders sitting in the open space in the gates of the town, accept that some food may not be eaten (perhaps not so difficult for us to appreciate – though for the wrong reasons; we wouldn't eat horse meat or tadpoles, after all; it's just that we happen to like pork and lobster), and avoid imposing modern western ideas upon the biblical society (supposing that circumcision was introduced for hygienic purposes, and that pork was off the menu because it was easily infected with germs and so a danger to health).

The Imagination already active

'What,' my readers begin to ask, 'has all this to do with preaching with imagination?' Just this. Once we begin to glimpse the difference between the Bible and ourselves, we may become open to the activity of the imagination. For we have begun to use that imagination already. One of my lecturers when I was an undergraduate urged us to 'let the modern European fabric of [our] daily vision fade far away, dissolve, be quite forgot'. 'Notes,' he declared, 'are often necessary, but they are necessary evil.' Rather, we should join ourselves for a little while to the sons and daughters of Jerusalem, determining that their people shall be our people, and their God our God.[5] Then, when we have joined ourselves with the people of old and come to think their thoughts, fear their fears, and rejoice with them that do rejoice, we shall look back to our own land, now perhaps itself become a trifle strange, and imagination will have a chance to mould our thoughts.

3

DIALOGUE WITH THE TEXT

An alleged Chinese proverb is said to declare: 'If you want to know what water is don't ask a fish.' Often it is only by looking at a different culture that we see our own with clear vision. To travel to the strange world of the Bible is one of the most valuable ways in which imagination can bring fresh understanding to the Christian message. But this can only happen if we recognise its strangeness.

Ephesians 5:21-6:9; Colossians 3:18-4:6

Changes in social customs and attitudes mean that often imagination calls us to travel the long distance between our own land and that strange land of the Bible and enter into dialogue with the text. And sometimes the Lectionary forbids us to do so. Looking down the index of the *Revised Common Lectionary* we find two holes where Ephesians 5:21-6:9 and Colossians 3:18-4:6 ought to be. Yet when the imagination plays on these two passages we can discover a great deal about the way we should approach the Bible as well as about personal relationships.

When our grandchildren visit us we sometimes play Happy Families with them using a very ancient set of cards that have somehow survived. The names are intriguing. Mr Cane, the schoolmaster. Mr Measure, the milkman – in a horse float. Schoolteachers are no longer permitted to cane their 'students', and milk has to be hygienically sealed in bottles or cartons, not drawn out of the churn with a pint measure and poured into the waiting jug. There are other changes that are not marked on the playing cards. George Henry Lewes could not divorce his wife, despite her repeated adultery and the fact that their marriage had completely broken down. So he and George Eliot had to 'live in sin'.[1] Thomas Hardy notes that the Matrimonial Causes Act of 1857 permitted a husband to divorce his wife for adultery alone, but the wife had to prove not only her husband's adultery but that he had aggravated the situation by such conduct as grievous cruelty. In *The Woodlanders*, Grace could not obtain a divorce from Fitzpiers because he had not been cruel enough. As Grace's father bluntly puts it: 'He has not done you *enough* harm! You are still subject to his beck and call.'[2] Imagination must work extremely hard if we are to enter that world of only a century and a half ago. Today, divorce is straightforward and available to everyone, and more and more couples decide to live together without getting married. 'Single parents' now are rarely widows or widowers. 'Partner' is almost driving out 'wife' and 'husband' from our language (listen to the nurses' embarrassment and uncertainty as they talk to patients and their visitors).

Given the changes that have occurred in so short a time, it should not surprise us that Paul's admonitions to husbands and wives, parents and children, masters and slaves appear not just old-fashioned but almost grotesque. 'So leave them out,' says the Lectionary. 'Not so,' imagination retorts, and asks us to work out what belongs simply to Paul's society, and what needs to be ferried across to our own world. Perhaps the most striking feature is the way Paul (or whoever wrote Ephesians) presses beyond the barrier formed by what is permitted to what is possible for Christians who are inspired by the love they have seen in Christ. If Paul remains a man of his age in calling on wives to be subject to their husbands, he goes beyond the age by urging husbands to love their wives as much as Christ loved the Church. If children are to obey their parents, fathers are not to provoke their children to anger. If slaves are to be obedient to their masters and serve them with a good will, masters are not to threaten their slaves but to remember that they are equal to them before their Master in heaven. 'To go the second mile' partly expresses this, but because it has become a dead metaphor, worn out by constant reiteration and squeezed into a proverb, imagination demands that we look elsewhere for illumination. In one of Jesus' parables, the generous farmer asks: 'Am I not allowed to do what I choose with what belongs to me?' It is an assertion which usually is made to justify our selfishness. The farmer uses it to defend his generosity.

After Paul left Corinth

Sometimes the preacher is presented with the reverse of this. It was the biblical world that was changing. Bruce W Winter has examined the way the problems which Paul had to face in his first letter to the church in Corinth were caused partly because many of the Christians were acting in secular ways, and partly because four social changes had recently occurred: the establishing of the imperial cult, the moving of the site of the Isthmian Games, three severe grain shortages, and the ending of the supply of kosher meat in the public market.[3] These were events that happened after Paul had left Corinth, so he had to think out afresh what it meant to live as a Christian in changing social conditions. The problems were not ones that he had anticipated while he was there.

'Look at the way the Church, chameleon-like, reflects the ideas of surrounding society,' says imagination. 'Ask what features of church life and religious thought have been imported into the Church. And don't forget to notice the way legal changes affect such things as the employment of church caretakers and the provision of food on church premises.'

Cutting the animals in half

One of the more curious passages included in the Lectionary is Genesis 15:1-18. If ever there were a passage that takes us to the heart of strangeness it must be this.

Not many in our congregations will have come to church expecting to hear about Abram chopping some animals in half. Imagination might sidetrack the preacher into wondering why they *have* come, and that might be a way of 'moving beyond the text' as the title of the next chapter has it. But suppose imagination holds the preacher firmly to the text. What of that heifer, goat, ram, turtle-dove and pigeon? The ritual must have been hidden in the distant past at the time the Old Testament was written down, perhaps not understood even by this writer as he formed the Hebrew letters on the papyrus or parchment. And the words of God, 'Fear not, Abram, I am your shield', might be true for Abram, who would get a son and have descendants that now number many millions, but it will not feel like that to the mother of a child drowned on a school outing, or the husband of a young teacher killed by a lorry as she cycled to school. If God is a shield, the shield is not a defence which prevents suffering. And those animals. Cutting them in half and walking between the halves seems to have been an ancient way of securing a covenant, firmer than a promise, more solemn than a vow. God pledged himself to be faithful to Abraham. The animals were killed. They had no say. They could not refuse. The preacher may travel swiftly to the victim who *chose* the cross as his way of ratifying the promise of God's love. Yet familiar as the cross is to Christians, it is not part of our workaday life. Terrorists and slaves are not crucified today. Imagination uses the weird story of Abram to startle the preacher into an awareness of the strangeness of the cross, and the traditional theology that has been developed from it.

The strangeness concealed

By its omissions (necessary but unfortunate) the Lectionary conceals much of the strangeness of the Bible. The set verses from Leviticus 19 (1-2, 9-18) consist of the call to be holy because Yahweh is holy and a set of ethical commandments, leading up to 'You shall love your neighbour as yourself.' Commentators point out that all of the Ten Commandments can be found within the chapter and are joined to specific provisions to provide security for the poor. It is only when the whole chapter is read that its strangeness strikes us. It contains both ethical and ritual laws, and these are intermixed without any sense that there is any difference between them. All are God's commands. Alongside the prohibitions of stealing, dealing falsely, lying, robbery and oppression, and the call to leave gleanings for the poor and pay workmen their wages each evening, are laws forbidding the wearing of clothes made from mixed material, sowing fields with two different kinds of seed, not eating meat with the blood in it, cutting the hair and the beard in particular ways, and tattooing. Any meat left over from a sacrifice for more than two days must be destroyed. The fruit from the first three years after a tree has been planted is described as 'uncircumcision' (literally 'foreskin') and is not to be eaten.

The usual explanation is that the Israelites had not yet learned to distinguish between ethical and ritual requirements. Both were thought to be displeasing to God. It is more probable that *all* the commandments were thought of as concerned with purity. God is holy. His people must be holy. To us it might seem that impurity was treated as a 'sin'. The reverse is probably how the ancient Israelites viewed it. To break the ethical norms is a form of impurity. So stealing is not merely a crime. It impairs the holiness of Israel before the holy God. When this is realised, ethics are transformed.

Imagination then looks for ways in which the preacher can open the text of the Lectionary to the congregation and reveal the transcendent holiness of God that calls his people to a like holiness. It will prevent the preacher from an arid moralising that is not softened by the gentle rain of religion.

4

MOVING BEYOND THE TEXT

Jonah

Sometimes the Lectionary offers only a snippet of a book that demands to be read as a whole. Jonah is one such book. The set extracts come only from chapters 3 and 4, obviously focusing on God's mercy and his acceptance of the repentance of the inhabitants of Nineveh. The preacher's platitudes dribble out of even the best of the notes and commentaries on the Lectionary readings. Imagination invites the preacher to present the whole of this marvellous fairy story, with the boat that thinks it will break up, the giant fish specially prepared for Jonah, the people of Nineveh all putting on sackcloth, even the animals – can we picture the sheep, goats and cows in their little sacking shifts? – and the Jack-and-the-beanstalk plant, the 'son of a night', that grows in a night and withers in a night. There is the angry Jonah: when God forgives the Ninevites and does not destroy the city, he breaks out with: 'Just what I said! I knew you would be soft and let them off. That's why I didn't want to preach to them.' There is the Jonah of inconsistent faith – he can trot out his creed when challenged by the sailors: 'I fear the LORD, the God of heaven, who made the sea and the dry land', and yet he has tried to sail off to Tarshish to escape from this God! There are the sailors, more religious than the Lord's prophet, and with a higher sense of right and wrong, refusing to cast Jonah into the sea, and exerting all their strength to row back to land – and then offering a prayer before they finally throw Jonah overboard. Imagination suggests approaching the book with a light touch, and sees in it a gospel close to that of the New Testament. The preacher might even consider the Jonah that lurks inside each one of us – confident in our creed, feeling superior to men and women of other religions and none. And in these days the statement by God that ends the book has a special poignancy.

Esther

Another book of which the Lectionary only allows us to glimpse a fragment is Esther. It is not clear what it intends preachers to pick out of the 11 verses, but they are very likely to pass by such a tiny segment of the book and preach on one of the other readings for the day. As with all stories, the meaning is in the whole. Yet the whole does not at first seem promising, with its accounts of planned genocide, harems and vindictive reprisals, set in a man's world where women must be kept under lest they rise up in revolt and refuse to obey their husbands. Worse, it lacks any single mention of God. Even the Greek translators were shocked and introduced God and prayer into the book to make it more 'religious'.

Imagination invites the preacher to begin by asking whatever a book like this is doing in the Bible, perhaps quoting Luther: 'I am so hostile to this book and to Esther that I could wish that they did not exist at all, for they Judaize too greatly and have much pagan impropriety.'[1] But Sherlock Holmes found significance in the dog that didn't bark. Perhaps, whispers imagination, there is a message in the absence of the name of God in the book. This might lead into a discussion of the activity of God when we cannot see him. Or the book can present a challenge to faith in a world that is ambiguous about truth, goodness and God.

Job

The few readings from the book of Job present the preacher with even greater problems. The 'semi continuous' reading in Year B offers 1:1 + 2:1-10; 23:1-9, 16-

17; 38:1-7, (34-41) and 42:1-6, 10-17 for the four Sundays in October. The 'related' readings link 'I know that my Redeemer liveth' (Job 19:23-27*a*) with Luke 20:27-38 (Proper 27, Year C) and Job 38:1-11 with Mark 4:35-41 in Year B. But like Jonah, Esther (and Ruth) Job makes sense only when the book is read as a whole. The emphasis on the narrative framework in the 'semi-continuous' reading is especially harmful in that it distorts the intention of the author. How, then, can the preacher move beyond the text? A lively imagination will find many ways.

The message of the book might be explored on the first Sunday, taking the set reading as no more than a point of departure. Again, imagination will eschew a bald outline of the book, and will look for a way to indicate what the writer is attempting to do:

> My mother was a nurse, so I suppose I ought to have been aware of illness and suffering. I was not. What struck me more than anything else when I went as a young minister to my first church was the amount of suffering I encountered in my visiting. A young boy had been brain damaged at birth. A woman had a stroke, and I saw her, week after week, in bed, paralysed, often crying, always complaining. A young man had been sent home to die: his bed was soaked with an open cancer, while his wife tried to look after him and cope with their two children. The husband of one keen church member had lost one arm and the other hand in the First World War; he depended utterly on his wife – and then his wife died. It was impossible not to ask, Why?

The sermon would then take the book of Job as a starting-point to discuss the problem, which is as real today as it was in the time when Job was written.

Alternatively, the imagination might draw a contrast between the way we would be likely to be presented with the problem today and the way the writer of Job dealt with it.

We switch on the television and a programme on suffering has just begun. We are shown a series of rapid shots of many different kinds of pain – a cancer patient, a child wounded in Palestine, the victims of a road accident, an aged and senile patient in a home, hungry people in Africa, the dead and wounded in two world wars. There are black and white shots of Auschwitz and Hiroshima. Stark numbers of those killed in wars shriek out from the screen. Then we are introduced to a panel of 'experts': a psychologist, a philosopher, a sociologist, a novelist. Curiously there is no theologian. They argue the case.

It is quite different with Job. Rather like a Conrad novel, where a moral issue is presented though the experience of one man,[2] the writer of Job seems to say: 'If you want to understand suffering, look at Job.'

This would then lead into an account of Job's wrestling with doubt and an absent God.

With both of these approaches the Job readings on the subsequent Sundays would be simply introduced with a brief comment, while the sermon would be based on one or other of the texts, since the whole book had already been the subject of the sermon.

There are many other ways in which the problem posed by the snippets from Job might be tackled. The preacher might look in turn at 'The patient Job', 'The impatient (or angry) Job', 'The incomprehensible God', and 'Did the author get it wrong?' These sermons would be more closely connected with the readings, although each would move well beyond the readings themselves.

Imagination might take a different line. Suppose the book of Job is not concerned with the problem of suffering but rather with the question of the relation between human beings and God. The Job sermon may then be left until the second or even the fourth Sunday. It might begin like this:

> Job relied on his own goodness. He was confident in his integrity – however powerfully his sufferings might seem to deny it and whatever his friends assert. But he cannot understand. It seems as if God has become his enemy – a spy, looking for the least peccadillo that he may commit, so that he can punish him. He even appears to delight in destroying innocent and guilty alike. Yet Job cannot believe this. The heart of his problem is that God seems to have hidden himself. 'Behold, I go forward, but he is not there; and backward, but I cannot perceive him; on the left hand I seek him, but I cannot behold him; I turn to the right hand, but I cannot see him.' If only he could reach God and set out his defence he is confident that all would be well.
>
> The climax comes in chapter 31. In a great oath of clearance, Job declares that he is free from falsehood, adultery, ill-treatment of his slaves, hardness towards the poor. He is free of sins of thought as well as action. And it is all absolutely true. So he strides into God's presence like a prince. This record deserves an acquittal that can be worn as a crown.

The preacher will stress the goodness of Job, goodness which even the Satan cannot fault and which God acknowledges. But Job has totally misunderstood what religion is all about. No one can stride into God's presence like a prince, setting out his record and claiming that it deserves to be worn as a crown. It is only after he has seen the incomparable splendour of the transcendent God that Job discovers at last what true religion is.

The 'related readings' do not present quite the same difficulty. The preacher can fasten on the 'afterlife' of Job 19, possibly drawing on Handel's aria, and ignoring both the textual difficulties of the famous verse and the fact that the 'redeemer' is the next of kin whose responsibility it is to buy back land that would otherwise have been sold out of the family, and avenge his death. In this the imagination fastens on the afterlife of the text.[3] Job 38:1-11 offers the opportunity to enable the congregation to see God's glory from within our cramped and dreary materialistic age. I look at this in chapter 11.

5

GOING AGAINST THE TEXT

'Paul got this quite wrong'

Large numbers of people attend Evensong in Westminster Abbey, most of them visitors, some encountering Christian worship for the first time. To make the Bible readings more accessible the readers introduce them with one or two sentences. One day the Dean, Edward Carpenter, was the reader, the reading 1 Corinthians 14:26-40, in which Paul declares that women should remain silent in church, for, wrote Paul, it is shameful for them to speak. In his introduction the Dean said: 'St Paul got this quite wrong'. Trevor Beeson, who recounts the incident, comments: 'It was a brave assertion, but left unanswered my question: If St Paul was mistaken, why read his erroneous words in Evensong?'[1] The *Revised Common Lectionary* answers Beeson's question by omitting it from the Sunday lessons.

This I regret, for it deprives the preacher of an opportunity to face up to the strange land of the Bible, and the extent to which social custom controlled even the great apostle's thinking. It also takes away the chance of discussing such important issues as the place of the Bible in determining Christian ethics, and the authority which it is to be accorded. These are vital issues which affect the everyday life of the Christian. No doubt there are other ways of approaching them and other texts which will provide the door, but the Dean's bald statement, perhaps quoted in a service where the reading had been followed by 'This is the word of the Lord', offers an opening for the imagination that can hardly be improved upon.

There are other passages where imagination may possibly persuade the preacher to go against the text.

Acts 9:1-6

It is the Fourth Sunday of Easter in Year C. The first reading is Acts 9:1-6, that we are allowed to continue to verse 20 if we wish: Luke's account of the way Jesus appeared to Paul as he travelled to Damascus.

Paul's conversion is so imprinted on the Christian consciousness that everyone is expected to have a similar experience – especially Methodists, who are never allowed to forget that day when John Wesley felt his heart 'strangely warmed'. Many Christians can give the exact time and place when they dedicated themselves to Christ.

Hugh Montefiore, the former Bishop of Birmingham, certainly could. He describes the time when he was sitting in his study in Rugby School, a normal 16 year old schoolboy, not thinking about anything in particular, when suddenly he became aware of a figure in white and he heard the words 'Follow me'. Somehow he knew it was Jesus. He became a Christian as a result of that totally unexpected and most unusual spiritual experience. At the time he was not dissatisfied with the Judaism into which he had been born. He had never attended a Christian service. His Christian friends had not tried to convert him. He writes in his autobiography: 'People ask me why and when I decided to convert. I did not decide at all: it was decided for me.'[2]

The reading from Acts 9 and the account by the Bishop in his autobiography would appear to lead inevitably to a sermon on conversion. 'But,' imagination whispers, 'what about all those Christians who have never had a religious experience?' 'Try to enable them to have one,' replies the dreary, commonplace mind. 'But they are earnest, eager to help others, kind and devout,' imagination replies, 'surely you don't want to make them feel guilty or think that they are second-class Christians?' So imagination points the way to a sermon for those who have never received a religious experience. It will not try to work them up into having one. It will fasten on Montefiore's strong affirmation that the experience which came to him was totally unexpected. Those who have received such experiences have done nothing to earn them or make them happen. 'He appeared to me,' Paul wrote, with evident surprise, in one of his letters (1 Corinthians 15:8-10). So imagination will lead us away from the text, to explore a faith that is *not* grounded on a vivid experience of God. It will point to the way these believers live 'as if God exists', offering worship Sunday by Sunday, kneeling in prayer even if the words seem to be going into the void, living the kind of life that a God of love would desire. 'What faith!' we often say of the man or woman who has been battered by life and yet has no doubts at all about God or his love. Imagination leads us to say the same words of those who are faithful to the Christian way even though they have never had any religious experience.

'Difficult' texts

The preacher's reaction to Paul's Damascus Road experience may be ambiguous: should he or she go along with the text and fasten on conversion, or should they, as I have suggested here, allow imagination to oppose it? Sometimes, however, imagination will demand that the preacher should oppose the text in an even more forthright way. Most of such 'difficult' texts have been filtered out of the Bible by the Lectionary, either by omitting the offending verses or leaving the passage out altogether. In this it goes beyond the earlier Lectionary compiled by the Joint Liturgical Group. The Fall of Jericho is no longer read. John's account of the occasion when Jesus said to 'the Jews', 'You are of your father the devil', has been deleted from the Lectionary's canon. Deuteronomy has been carefully edited to remove any mention of the call to utterly destroy all the Canaanites who have been defeated in Yahweh's war against them, putting men, women and children to death; it leaves a much kinder and more appealing book. But some difficulties remain.

Genesis 22:1-14

The compilers of the Lectionary managed to delete God's commands to carry out genocide against the Canaanites, but they found it impossible to omit Genesis 22:1-14, for its afterlife in both Judaism and Christianity has given it an assured place in religious thought. The story is so familiar, so beautifully told, that the horror of the situation is eased. Perhaps it is for these reasons that the congregation listens as it is read with almost no reaction. Yet they ought to be shocked. What kind of a God is it who could test the extent of a man's obedience by requiring him to put his son to death? God may have planned to prevent the knife from being thrust into the young man's heart as he lay, bound and helpless, on the altar that his father had built; that does not make the test any less hideous. And in the narrative God does not halt the knife until it is actually raised above the boy.

The way out which we commonly take is to see in the story the prefiguring of that other sacrifice of a Son. In that other story, there was no ram to offer as a substitute, and the cry 'My God, why have you abandoned me?' received no answer. It is all right, we say, for unlike Isaac (and unlike the many animals sacrificed as offerings to God as a part of worship), this victim went willingly. He *chose* to die for the sins of the world. That is one way, the easy way.

The writer of the Letter to the Hebrews sees in the story a model for total faith and trust in God, and that is another, even easier, way to evade the horror of a God who asks a father to sacrifice his son to him.

Imagination will not allow us to follow it. For imagination bends our gaze back to Isaac and Sarah. Isaac, deceived by his father, who lacks the courage to answer his son's question, 'Where is the lamb of the burnt offering?' Sarah, who is not even mentioned in the Genesis account. The members of the preacher's congregation *ought* to be made to face these questions. They *ought not* to let the well known story run its course with an unthinking compliance.

It is not just modern readers who have been troubled by the story. When the Jewish author of the Book of Jubilees retold the story in the second century BC, he felt the need to make Satan, not God, initiate this test of Abraham. God only consents to it, in a way similar to the Book of Job. 'Prince Mastema [Satan] came and he said before God, "Behold, Abraham loves Isaac, his son. And he is more pleased with him than everything. Tell him to offer him [as] a burnt offering upon the altar. And you will see whether he will do this thing. And you will know whether he is faithful in everything in which you test him."'[3]

Then there is the forgotten Sarah. What were her feelings? And how are we to suppose Abraham extracted Isaac from his mother? Sebastian Brock has collected together some ancient Christian homilies which elaborate on the story.[4] Their concern about Sarah is striking. From the silence about Sarah the writers deduce that Abraham did not tell Sarah anything about what he was planning to do. In one fifth-century Syriac homily Sarah is suspicious right from the start. In another Sarah demands that Abraham should tell her where he is taking her son. Yet another makes Sarah remonstrate with Abraham and only let Isaac go with his father because she is under the impression that Isaac is going to assist in making a sacrifice to God, and is unaware that he is to be the victim. In most, however, Sarah's faith is seen to be equal to that of Abraham. In all this imagination has much to reflect upon.

The prophets

Perhaps we regard the prophets as fairly 'safe', and are at ease with their condemnation of various social sins which we proceed to transfer rather too readily to our own society, ignoring the chasm that exists between the economic structure of ancient Israelite society and our own. The ethics of the prophets cannot be directly applied to the modern world. But some features of the prophets' oracles should be of even greater concern to us. For here are found statements which we must either ignore (and hope our congregations haven't noticed them, or if they have, that they will not ask awkward questions about them) or confront the text. Consider:

> If you are willing and obedient,
>   you shall eat the good of the land;
> But if you refuse and rebel,
>   you shall be devoured by the sword;
>   for the mouth of the LORD has spoken.
>
> Isaiah 1:19-20

Do we really believe that God punishes disobedience by bringing a national enemy to destroy a nation?

Or take Amos. 'The Lord GOD showed me: behold, a basket of summer fruit. And he said, "Amos, what do you see?" And I said, "A basket of summer fruit." Then the LORD said to me, "The end has come upon my people Israel" ' (Amos 8:1). What would we say if a minister today announced God's judgement on the government by claiming that he had had a vision and that the message of the vision came through a pun?[5]

Once imagination has dragged us back to the world of Israel in the eighth or seventh centuries BC, it will have hard work attempting to vitalise the oracles of the prophets. The work will be worthwhile.

Noah's ark

It is the same problem as that we face with Noah's ark. In an attempt to link the Bible with the modern concern for endangered species of birds and mammals, it is not uncommon to portray the ark as a symbol of conservation. What is forgotten are the unpalatable words of God before the flood: 'I shall wipe off the face of the earth this human race which I have created – yes, man and beast, creeping things and birds. I regret I ever made them' (Genesis 6:7, REB). Noah may be the great conservationist, and God may instruct him to save every species by building the ark, but the disaster was produced directly by God himself, not by greenhouse gases that lead to global warming or by the destruction of the creatures' habitats. Here imagination works in a two-sided way, first directing the preacher's attention to what is actually written in the text, not what we wish were there, and secondly moving to an attempt to relate this to today – a task which is far more difficult than most of us suppose. N T Wright sees the flood as God's 'sober and proper reaction to human rebellion, neither capricious nor malevolent', and turns to salvation through Christ.[6] But imagination asks whether doctrine can be imported quite so simply.

Mark 13:24-37

The New Testament is not without its problems either. What is the preacher to do with Mark 13:24-37, the gospel reading for the First Sunday in Advent in Year B? Here is a passage whose strangeness cannot be missed. At its face value it describes the end of the world. There is total cosmic disintegration. The sun no longer shines. The moon gives no light. The stars fall from the sky. The Son of Man comes in clouds, sends out his angels, and collects those who have been chosen. The preacher who studies the commentaries will be able to trace the origins of these ideas and give this kind of writing a fancy name, but that will not be very helpful to the congregation. There is little in this passage that makes sense to us today. We do not believe, if we are honest, that the universe is going to disintegrate at any moment and Jesus will suddenly appear. Photographs of the earth taken by travellers to the moon, space probes to distant parts of the solar system, studies of distant galaxies provide our pictures of the universe, not the weird language of this chapter. 'Watch,' says Jesus at the end of the reading. He meant, 'Be ready for the sudden and imminent coming of the Son of Man.' Imagination presents a different kind of watching. This watching is to go beyond the clash of worldviews, and asks: 'How far is my life determined by secular pictures of the world and human behaviour rather than by my religious beliefs?' And that leads to other questions, such as: 'What place does prayer have in my life, when I find it difficult to evade the cause and effect that seem to run throughout the universe? How far am I open to biological reductionism, when I try to make sense of evolution and genetics? What does it mean to live as a Christian in a free-market economy?'

Mark 3:20-35

Then there are the demons. Mark 3:20-35 is the gospel reading for the Sunday between 5th June and 11th June in Year B. Some may be quite at ease with exorcism, asking only that it is carefully conducted by clergy specially trained for the task and properly appointed by the diocese. Others may direct our attention to the habit we all have of 'demonising' those who differ from us, jumping quickly from the first-century story to the practices of the 20th and 21st centuries. It is not greatly different from the common interpretation of Paul's 'principalities and powers' as the structural evils in society against which the Christian has to fight. Imagination requires us first of all to return to the strange world of first-century Palestine, where hostilities between different groups in Judaism were bitter and demons real, and then to travel back to our world of hospitals and science, the large-scale testing of powerful drugs, and the identification of faulty genes. Imagination will ask us if we are content to live in a capsule that protects us from the germs of the everyday world so that we can pretend to live in the world of the first century. If not, what then?

Living imaginatively within the biblical world, and then moving back to our own is not easy. Nevertheless, it is essential for the preacher.

6

RESTORING THE SPARKLE

I am told that somewhere in the writings of that odd humorist, P G Wodehouse, one of his characters speaks of 'that kind of story which you think you have understood, and suddenly it turns round and slaps your face'. Not being a devotee of Wodehouse, in spite of the fact that he once lived round the corner from my present home (the plaque on the house is so high up that you need binoculars to read it), and although I keep in my memory those curious TV pictures of him laboriously typing out his stories with one finger, seeming not to know where the next letter on the keyboard was, I do not know the context. But the description exactly expresses what a parable is. Read Nathan's parable of the ewe lamb and you will see this immediately. But when you know that the slap is going to come, you move your face out of the way. And we know this with every one of Jesus' parables. So preaching on the parables is one of the most difficult of the preacher's tasks.

Imaginative preaching looks beyond the run-of-the mill sermons on texts that have been worn smooth by their constant repetition and our over-familiarity with them. We know what the reader is going to say as soon as we hear the first sentence. Only imagination can retrieve the situation. But it must be a living imagination, and not an imagination which has grown old and feeble along with the parable.

The Good Samaritan

Take the parable of the Good Samaritan. When Jesus first told this parable it must have made an immense impact upon his hearers. A Samaritan, travelling along that dangerous road, came to where the man who had been robbed and left for dead was lying – and he went to him, bound up his wounds, brought him to the inn, paid for his keep, and promised to pay anything more when he came that way again. A Samaritan! The story was new: the climax astounding. But 'Good Samaritan' has become a dead metaphor, so often has the phrase been used, and we in the churches have heard the story so many times that we hardly pay attention to it any more. G B Caird once suggested that the children's riddle, 'What has eyes but cannot see?' is needed to make us aware that 'the eye of a needle' is a metaphor.[1] What then can imagination do with the parable of the Good Samaritan?

Perhaps, remembering an exercise that had been set us while we were at school, we try to breathe life into the worn-out story by providing a modern setting. Substitute new characters: a woman mugged and beaten up, lying in the gutter – a doctor, tired from his 60 hours on call in hospital and wondering whether the relatives will sue if he tries to revive the man and fails, and if this happens whether he will be covered by his insurance – a social worker, hurrying to the last of her clients who is threatening to commit suicide, and has too heavy a case-load – and a homosexual, who tries to stop the woman's bleeding, carries her to a safe place and calls 999. But imagination whispers, 'It won't work, you know. The congregation knows the story so well that the only interest will be in wondering what characters you will bring into the story. The impact of "Go and do likewise" will not be recovered.'

A different approach is suggested by Browning's *The Ring and the Book*.[2] Browning discovered a 'square old yellow book' on a stall in the market of San Lorenzo in Florence. It contained the account of a forgotten Roman murder case. By taking each of the characters in turn –

Count Guido Franceschini, Pompilia's husband, who was arrested for her murder; Guiseppe Caponsacchi, the 24 year old priest who accompanied Pompilia when she fled from her husband; Pompilia, as she lies dying after the murderous attack by her husband and his paid assassins; the defence and prosecuting lawyers; the aged Pope who has to decide whether to allow the count's appeal – Browning presents a searching exploration of guilt and innocence, truth and falsehood, and the motives that drive men and women. So the preacher might enter into the minds of the characters in the parable, telling in turn the story as recounted by the innkeeper, the Levite, the priest, the traveller, and maybe discovering that the Samaritan was a man of few words, who acted rather than spoke. It might just work.

An alternative might be to raid biography. The journalist may show us the way.[3] 'During Dr Matthew Lukwiya's funeral, the pallbearers wore face-masks, latex gloves and surgical gowns, and the restricted number of mourners pressed back from the tightly sealed coffin.' Matthew Lukwiya was one of the bravest men that we are ever likely to hear about. Seventy per cent of newly qualified Ugandan doctors move to lucrative practices in South Africa, Europe and the Middle East. The best ever student in tropical paediatrics at the school of tropical medicine in Liverpool, Matthew Lukwiya was so outstanding that he was offered a lecturing post in the university, and turned it down. Once qualified he headed back to an Italian missionary hospital outside Gulu in the region of his own people. He was on leave at the University of Kampala when three student nurses died, all bleeding or vomiting blood. Lukwiya sat up all night going over the unexplained deaths. He became convinced that it was ebola, a highly infectious viral fever. There is no cure. Many of the doctors at the hospital took their families and fled. Lukwiya did not hesitate. He went back. He took care. Wore all the protective clothing – except once, when a half-crazed, dying nurse started thrashing about, spraying blood and vomit, and in his haste Lukwiya didn't put on his goggles. They buried him beneath the leafy mango trees and bright bougainvillaea in the grounds of Lucor. 'He knew the risk,' said his widow. 'He saw that he was needed for his patients and he did it.'

There is a third way. It must now be almost 50 years since I sat in a chapel in Cambridge and heard the minister describe how, when he was a missionary in China, he was going along a desolate mountain road and came upon what he thought at first was a bundle of old clothes. Then he realised it was a man. He had obviously been attacked by the bandits who were known to hide out in the hills and swoop down suddenly on travellers. He anxiously looked round. Was this a trap set by the bandits? Were they in hiding close by? The man looked dead anyway. The minister hurried on. It electrified the congregation.

Not many of us can make a parable come alive in that way, and few of us would be prepared to admit that we had once been the priest or the Levite. Yet this might be a way to present that other all too hackneyed parable, the Sheep and the Goats. For years preachers have lambasted their congregations, often most unfairly, for not following the teaching of Jesus in this parable. In fact every survey that has been carried out shows that churchgoers give far more to charities than their non-worshipping fellow citizens, and a far higher percentage of them engage in some form of social service. Many people in our congregations are doing these things, often as secretly and unawares as the sheep in the parable. Yet very few of us would have the courage of Matthew Lukwiya. Certainly I haven't. What, then, about the things that Jesus lists in this other parable? The trouble is I know myself too well. To be honest, I am just not prepared to welcome drop-outs and drug-users into my home. I don't know how to start challenging the things in society which produce drop-outs and drug-users. And my personality makes some things impossible to me; if I attempted them I should only do them badly. So I must resign myself to being a goat. I see imagination nodding approval of this approach.[4]

The Lost Sheep and the Lost Coin

Another set of parables that are likely to defeat all but the most imaginative of preachers is the group in Luke 15, the lost sheep, the lost coin, and the prodigal son. The Lectionary includes the first two on the Sunday between 11th September and 17th September. We slot in the 'meaning' without even having to think. Commentators wonder what they can say about something that is so obvious. So they try to add colour by filling in the background. They point to the risk of leaving 99 sheep in the desert while hunting for the lost one. They describe the shepherd, worn out after the trek across the barren hills, straining to lift the sheep onto his shoulders. It may help to put a little life into the dehydrated parables, but more commonly we lazily interpret them in the light of the Pauline doctrine of justification through the death of Christ and leave it there. Both parables end with a reference to 'one sinner who repents'. The trouble is that there is little sign that the sheep repented of its escapade, and repentance seems an impossibility for a hard and unfeeling coin.

It may help if we look at the way Luke has put the first two parables side by side and within a frame. One parable is about a man, the other about a woman. The man is relatively wealthy and works in the open air: the woman is poor and confined to the house. If we are going to fill in the background with picturesque details from Palestine, we should fill in the social background as well. As for the frame that Luke constructs, it presents the parables as a defence of the way Jesus 'receives sinners and eats with them', emphasises the joy God has at finding what has been lost, and links that joy with the repentance of the sinners.

Perhaps when imagination forces us to think about the passage, we shall come to the conclusion that Luke was both right and wrong in the frame in which he set the parables. Right in seeing Jesus as defending the way he was happy to mix with the outcasts of the society in which he lived. Right in placing the main emphasis on the joy that he (and God) has when those outcasts enjoy his company as much as he enjoys theirs. Perhaps right again in stressing the effort that God makes to 'find' his lost children. But surely wrong when he claims that God's joy depends upon those children first repenting of their sin. Simply to want to be with him is sufficient.

Through the eyes of a blind man

Sometimes imagination calls us to approach the Bible from a different angle from that to which we are accustomed. John M Hull, Professor of Religious Education in the University of Birmingham, who lost the sight of one eye when he was quite young and finally lost the sight in the other eye 38 years later, approaches the Bible as a blind man. His insights (how our language implies that we live in a sighted world!) have much to offer to the preacher, for they can transform our understanding. It is also a test of the strength of our imagination. To what extent are we able to enter imaginatively into the world of the blind? Hardly at all, for we are so dominated by sight. We need Professor Hull to enable us to imagine what blindness is. When you are blind, things only exist if you can hear or touch them. Wind is real – you can hear it and feel it against your face. Clouds don't exist because they make no sound. People are names and voices. They suddenly come into existence when they speak, and suddenly go away when they stop. You don't know whether they are still there or not. It is impossible to go across a crowded room to speak to a friend. Stairs are not dangerous to a blind person – all are the same height, and there is usually a handrail. But approaching a staircase the blind person needs not just to know that she is coming to a flight of stairs; she needs to know whether they are going up or down.[5]

Once we have entered, however feebly, into the world of the blind person, we are ready to appreciate the Bible in entirely new ways.

Professor Hull believes that blindness as a metaphor for corruption, wickedness and sin, which runs through the Bible, has caused untold distress to blind people. Even some of the sayings of Jesus are spoken by a sighted person to sighted persons: the Jewish leaders are 'blind guides to the blind', the unhealthy eye makes the whole body full of darkness. It is the *wide* gate which is difficult for blind persons; they can touch the sides of the narrow gate and know exactly where they are.

What then about the story of blind Bartimaeus? Imagination invites us to consider an incident from Professor Hull's home life. He was putting his young son Thomas to bed and the following startling conversation took place:

'Will you always be blind?'
'Yes, always.'
'When did it happen?'
'It was before you were born.'
'Couldn't the doctors stop it?'
'The doctors tried.'
'Couldn't they do any more at the end? What did they say?'
'Well, they just said, "We're very sorry, Mr Hull, we are afraid there isn't much more we can do now." '
'That was bad luck. Why doesn't God help you?'
'He does help me, in lots of ways.'
'How?'
'Well, he makes me strong. He gives me courage.'
'But he doesn't help you to get your eyes back.'
'No, but he does help me with lots of other things.'

Thomas' questions prevent the congregation from giving an easy answer to the problem of suffering. Perhaps we might link it to 2 Corinthians 12:9.

Hull suggests that the writer of Psalm 139 shows such a deep understanding of blindness that he wonders whether the writer was blind. The psalmist is surprised that God can know at a distance (v2). Physical contact is important (v5), and God's 'hand' leads him. What is 'high' is beyond the experience of the blind (v6). No one can turn out the lights on a blind person: darkness and light are both alike (v11-12). We recall the picture of the blind harpist that the archaeologists have revealed to us.

Turn now to Hebrews 11: 'Faith is the assurance of things hoped for, the conviction of things not seen'. Although blindness is not mentioned in the chapter, the writer does not take sight for granted, and the blind person, for whom only those things within his or her reach materially exist, can appreciate the point far better than those of us who can see the stars and look out over the countryside from the tops of the hills. 'Faith . . . is the conviction of things not seen' now takes on a richer meaning.

To listen to the Bible through the sightless eyes of Professor Hull is to become sensitive to blind persons in a fresh way (and that is a good thing in itself) and to discover new meanings in many worn-out texts.

Looking closely at the text

If adopting a fresh way of looking at the text is one way to finding a new, imaginative understanding, looking closely at what is actually written is another.

It is Palm Sunday and we all know what to expect. Even if the children do not enact the Entry of Jesus into Jerusalem, we shall sing 'All glory laud and honour', 'Ride on, ride on in majesty', or perhaps 'Trotting, trotting'. But what about Year C, with its gospel, Luke 19:28-40. Because we are so used to harmonising the gospels we may overlook the fact that here is 'Palm Sunday' without any palm branches! To observe this might lead into a discussion of the way Luke tells the familiar story – so familiar that we did not notice the absence of the palm branches until imagination pointed it out – and then ask ourselves what Luke wishes to express through his way of telling the story.

7

ON NOT DESTROYING THE GLORY OF THE TEXT

The greatest problems for the preacher do not lie in the 'difficult passages' of the Old Testament or the 'hard sayings' of Jesus. Unless we maintain an ultra-conservative attitude towards the Bible, these texts can be highly stimulating. And in any case the Lectionary has filtered out the harshest of them as it offers us a bowdlerised Bible, so that neither we nor our congregations need be aware that they even exist.

It is the finest passages which are the hardest to preach on and which present the preacher with the greatest challenge of all. What is more destructive of all that worship should be than to take a passage, which, through its language and imagery, enables the congregation to think magnificently about God, and then to annihilate those thoughts through uninspired comments, trite opinions or banal language? Many a time the congregation must wish that instead of a sermon that brought down a mist on the grandeur of the biblical vista and shrouded the splendour of the text in a leaden cloud, they had been allowed to listen to that reading again, gazing in wonder at the eternal mystery of the divine.

How, then, can the preacher offer illumination on what already shines brightly? Here a sensitive imagination alone can bring help. For some preachers imagination is sufficiently alert that no other helps are needed than simply to read and reread the passage. They will almost instinctively see how its splendour can be enhanced. For most of us, though, a stimulus is needed to get the imagination going.

1 Kings 19:1-21

Sometimes the imagination of a scholar can rouse us from our theological slumbers. Take 1 Kings 19:1–21. ' "The LORD was not in the wind . . . not in the earthquake . . . not in the fire" – *'but he ought to have been'* writes Professor Robert Davidson. Wind, earthquake and fire were 'recurring symbols of God's mysterious presence in story and in psalm'. Now the symbols have failed. Listen to Professor Davidson again: 'It was as if the traditional symbols, which had once conveyed the reality of God's presence, had been emptied, left meaningless, no longer able to bear the burden of God's presence, no longer able to speak.'[1] Imagination carries us into the present. Often today the traditional Christian symbols that brought God close to generations of our ancestors fail us. Candles have become commonplace. The ancient liturgies in a special religious language have been replaced by words supposed to be more intelligible – and the sense of awe has gone. Even the cross has become a neon sign on the church alongside other shop signs, and the horror – and the glory – has departed. Keats described the way scientific knowledge had driven the magic from the rainbow:[2]

> There was an awful rainbow once in heaven;
> We know her woof, her texture; she is given
> In the dull catalogue of common things.

But wait. Although the traditional symbols failed Elijah, God was not absent. After the wind, the earthquake and the fire there came – what? – 'a still, small voice', 'a gentle whisper', 'a vibrant silence'. The translators are puzzled. How is the Hebrew to be translated? Professor Davidson thinks that the phrase points to 'a kind of silence so intense that you can hear it'. And in that silence Elijah found God again. 'The Lord's puzzling absence was the prelude to his surprising presence.' Imagination then asks the preacher to find where today God's surprising presence can be found.

Perhaps nowhere. For, as Ann Lewin expresses it, prayer is like watching for the kingfisher; all we can do is to be where he is likely to appear and wait.[3]

Isaiah 6

One of the most impressive chapters in the Old Testament is Isaiah 6, but as with other great masterpieces, preachers have reduced it to the commonplace by narrowing it to a demand for evangelism ('Here am I, send me'), or using it to convey conventional concepts of sin and forgiveness. A sojourn in the strange land of the Bible may enable us to avoid the most deadening expositions, though we shall never be able to match its rich imagery and numinous splendour.

The vision of Isaiah goes against most of the things we find in our daily life – and many of the things we find in our churches. Isaiah's God is quite different from the picture that lies behind our cosy prayers that begin, 'Dear Lord, we just want to thank you for all your love.' Isaiah's reaction to his vision of God is a sense of utter desolation, far removed from our easy confession of sin that takes an easy forgiveness as a matter of course. Isaiah's message is almost a call of despair: the people will never understand, they will never turn back to God and be healed, and the prophet must keep on proclaiming his message until God has devastated the land. It all sounds very odd when placed alongside the attempts of many churches today to be popular and turn worship into entertainment.

So imagination might lead us to turn to Rudolf Otto in order to fill out the idea of the numinous.[4] The English translations might be visited to show how most fail to express Isaiah's sense of uncleanness. The trouble is that we have lost the sense of purity, and the *Good News Bible,* despite its splendid, 'There is no hope for me! I am doomed', goes on to think of sin rather than uncleanness with its laboured: 'every word that passes my lips is sinful and I live among a people whose every word is sinful.' At the heart of Isaiah's response to his vision of God is an awareness of the gulf between the glory of God and the grubbiness of his life. A hymn may just enable us to catch a glimpse of this:[5]

Eternal Light! Eternal Light!
  How pure the soul must be;
When, placed within Thy searching sight,
It shrinks not, but, with calm delight,
  Can live, and look on Thee!

As for the futility of the task to which Isaiah is called – to keep on speaking to a people who are unable to understand what God is saying – we may find a counterpart in the way the world is rushing to environmental catastrophe, heedless of the warnings of the scientists, dulled by the politicians' quest for annual increases in economic production, which means destroying more of the planet in this futile enterprise of making more and more objects that diminish rather than enhance the quality of human life.

Colossians 3:12-17

Some passages in the New Testament are even more impossible. The Epistle for the first Sunday after Christmas in Year C of the *Revised Common Lectionary* is Colossians 3:12-17. Everyone in the congregation agrees with every word of it! The preacher is tempted, therefore, to chastise them for not doing what they agree with when they are in church. Imagination is appalled. Suppose we contrast Paul's exhortation with the common view that goodness means keeping the rules. I once began a sermon on this text like this: 'I told a lie once. Well, I probably have told lies many times, but this is one time that I remember after 53 years. I was in Suffolk. The hunters and the pack of hounds came into the field by the side of the road where I was cycling. "Have you seen the fox?" one of the hunters called out. In fact I had watched the fox rapidly crossing the field before the hunters and the dogs came over the brow of the hill. "No!" I replied.' This led into a sermon in which obeying the commandments was contrasted with 'putting on' the virtues which Paul describes, and, I hope, on the way making those virtues attractive.

1 Corinthians 13

How can the preacher preach on 1 Corinthians 13? It seems impossible. The power lies in the brevity of the descriptions of love. To try to expand on them will kill them in a long, lingering death of banality. Nothing can take the place of: 'Love is patient and kind; love is not jealous or boastful; it is not arrogant or rude . . .' What is the preacher to do?

Possibly the most imaginative thing would be to go into the pulpit, read the passage, and then sit down and say nothing for 15 minutes! The trouble is that the congregation, conditioned to expect words and yet more words, would suppose the preacher was feeling ill.

I knew a preacher once who scoured every translation that he could lay his hands on, and then offered the varying translations to the congregation, phrase by phrase. I was only 18 at the time, but it was sufficiently imaginative for me still to remember what he did, even though I cannot recall the translations.

Perhaps a preacher with a vast stock of biography might set a person or an incident in a person's life alongside each description of love. It would not be easy to do this imaginatively, but well done it could be fascinating.

Art might come to our aid, if we could project a slide expressive of each description of love on a screen – probably without any more comment than the very briefest of explanations of what the pictures were about.

David H C Read began a sermon on the passage with: 'When I went back and read again through the first half of this chapter, I noticed something strange that had escaped me before. There's no religion in it – not a word about God, about Christ, about prayer, or about eternal life.'[6] Now there's an imaginative thought! (He went on to say that those in the know are aware that religious belief is 'hovering in the wings', that the chapter is part of a letter to a Christian church and is loaded with Christian theology. We might think of other ways of continuing.)

8

THE USE OF LITERATURE AND MUSIC

Poetry

The 1960s not only destroyed respect for the sermon but also drove out literary allusions. Before that iconoclastic destruction of so much that was good in society and that period of mockery at so many features of Christian worship that brought the congregation close to the presence of God, preachers often introduced the fragrant spices of poetry into their sermons. A couple of lines of a poem can, as we shall see later, bring a sermon to an effective close. A verse can compress tons of verbiage into a memorable diamond. An aphorism will stay in the mind, when the preacher's shapeless sentences have drooped and fallen to the ground. Quoting poetry has gone out of fashion. It is time to return to that kindly custom.

In a sermon on confession Charles Williams' 'At the "Ye that do truly" ' will remind the congregation that each individual stands alone before their God.[1] Williams imagines his wife and himself in church. Together they listened to the commandments and professed their common faith. But

> Now are our prayers divided, now
> Must you go lonelily, and I;
> For penitence shall disallow
> Communion and propinquity.

That one word 'lonelily' will continue to sound, even if the rest of the verse – or the sermon – wilts into silence.

For the more adventurous the meaning of the life of Christ might be illuminated by turning back to the Old Saxon poem, 'The Heliand'.[2] The poet retells the story in ways that the Saxons would understand, hoping to build the new faith upon the old. Because it would have been derogatory for Mary and Joseph to be serfs he depicts them as nobles. 'No room in the inn' is omitted! The Chieftain of mankind is born in David's hill-fort. The shepherds are turned into horse-servants, on guard outside the inn. Peter's boat becomes a 'high-horned ship', a northern long-boat. Jesus is represented as the personal lord to whom the Saxon warrior-companions owe lifelong loyalty. At his baptism the Spirit came 'like a powerful bird, a magnificent dove' and sat upon his shoulder, as the black ravens perched on Woden's shoulders. The passion is almost the account of the 'last stand', with the thanes defending their lord. But there is a tragic flaw – one of the thanes commits the unthinkable and is disloyal, and the rest run away. Imagination has much to play with here, not least the idea that Jesus has to become our own if he is to be our saviour.

Among other poems that illuminate the passion, specially valuable are 'The Vision of a Rood',[3] 'The Bludy Serk',[4] several of the poems of Studdert-Kennedy, such as 'The Suffering God' and 'The Sorrow of God',[5] and David Gascoyne's 'Ecce Homo'.[6] J A W Bennett discusses several of these, and others, in *Poetry of the Passion*, a treasure chest for the preacher.[7]

Sin is a subject which preachers are expected to deal with, yet how seldom do they manage to do so sensitively. A poem by Ogden Nash may help.[8] It is too long to quote more than a few lines, but these will, I hope, show how it can open up whole new ways of thinking. After noting the distinction between sins of commission ('what you are doing when you are doing something you ortant') he fastens on sins of omission ('not having done something you shuddha'). It is this second kind of sin which 'lays eggs under your skin', for they are the sins we never get any fun from committing.

You didn't get a wicked forbidden thrill
Every time you . . . forgot to pay a bill;
You didn't slap the lads in the tavern on the
  back and loudly cry Whee,
Let's all fail to write just one more letter before we
  go home, and this round of unwritten letters is on
  me.

As important as selecting just the right poem, or lines from a poem, is the way we introduce them. The bare 'as . . . wrote' may occasionally be sufficient where the build-up to the quotation has been rich and full. More often a more oblique approach is needed. To introduce 'The Vision of a Rood' we might begin: 'We travel to Scotland, to the parish church of Ruthwell in Dumfries. We get the key from a cottage up the road. On a stone cross, massive within the little church, in runic letters, is an inscription. The Presbyterians partly defaced it in 1647. It is a fragment of an Anglo-Saxon poem. To find the complete poem we have to journey south to Italy. Vercelli was a stopping place for English pilgrims on their way to Rome. In Vercelli is preserved the only surviving manuscript of the entire poem. How fragile an existence writings possessed before the invention of printing!' By this time the congregation is eager to know what the poem was.

Hymns

Occasionally the preacher can take a hymn to illuminate a text. This will be most effective if the hymn is modern and not well known. Fred Pratt Green's 'Hope Completes the Trilogy',[9] which has not found its way into many hymnbooks, is ideal for exploring the meaning of Christian hope, stressing as it does that hope is a strong, necessary and creative virtue. What preacher or congregation can fail to have their imaginations stimulated with fresh insight on hearing the lines:

For hopeless Love is blind with tears,
And hopeless Faith with rage.

I spoke earlier of the difficulty in preaching on the great passages in the Bible. In this hymn Fred Pratt Green shows us one way.

Biography

Biography equally can kindle the imagination, and it has the additional advantage that it tells the story of people who lived a human life alongside or before us, not just in printed words arranged on a page by the novelist's craft. Notice that I am not talking about illustrations. That is quite another matter and might merit a whole book in itself. After all, didn't William Sangster give us *The Craft of Sermon Illustration*?[10] No, our subject is imagination, and what we are trying to discover is the way biography and novels can awaken the preacher's imagination on the one hand, and how imagination can introduce snippets of biography or dialogue from a novel into the sermon.

Suppose the preacher is faced with the daunting Luke 21:25-36. The problems that these words cause (or should cause!) to the modern believer can be presented vividly by a reference to J H Oldham.

> Towards the end of his life, when he was ill with jaundice and found that the smallest physical effort, such as fetching a book or writing a letter, was exhausting, J H Oldham wrote to Kathleen Bliss. He wondered why the Church had never really faced up to the fact that Jesus and the apostles fully expected the kingdom of God to come immediately.[11]

This might well form the beginning of the sermon. It enables the preacher to direct the attention of the congregation to the problem that the blunt words of Jesus present to us today. Perhaps the GNB's 'Remember that all these things will take place before the people now living have all died' heightens the intensity. Nearly 1900 years have passed since Luke wrote that down. Oldham had even harsher things to say in the letter. The great architect of the World Council of Churches wrote: 'To believe that the relatively small handful of people who meet at Geneva or the Vatican make any serious difference to what happens in history is to read the *Listener* or the Sunday papers with your eyes shut.' Once the difficulty is set out so clearly, the preacher cannot evade it and the congregation will demand an answer.

Or suppose we wish to preach about honesty. Curiously we shall not find any biblical text which expresses precisely what we mean today by the term. There is the commandment, 'You shall not steal', and Paul writes, 'Let the thief no longer steal', but none of the meagre number of places where the AV has 'honest' or 'honestly' retains the term in later translations, for it appears that the Greek word did not have this meaning. In an age of winning rather than earning, when advertisers and politicians conceal as much as they dare, honesty often appears an old-world virtue. It is almost impossible to convince the girl at the counter that she has given you too much change! So honesty deserves to be promoted by the preacher.

We might return to a vanished world to show the congregation the extent to which one Christian was prepared to go in maintaining scrupulous honesty. Sir John W Laing, the head of the famous construction firm, once ordered a row of houses that were almost finished to be pulled down because they were substandard. That is the fact. Imagination, however, will not be satisfied with such a bald statement. The congregation must see the houses, hear Laing's sharp command. So it urges us to begin: 'The bricklayers had completed their work. The carpenters had put the windows into the holes that had been left in the walls. The roof was on, and the electricians had installed the wiring. The plasterers were ready to start their work on the walls. But a man in an old mac has just arrived and looks critically at the buildings. Suddenly he gives the peremptory order: "Pull them all down." John W Laing would not permit shoddy work, The cost of demolition and rebuilding would be considerable. But he was too straight to allow unwary buyers to purchase houses that his critical eye judged to be substandard. He had obtained his concern for high standards from a master mason, who was as careful a hundred feet off the ground, where only the birds could see his work, as with the facing stones of the main entrance. "If I get shoddy over my work at one hundred feet," he said, "I might get into a slovenly way altogether." So the houses came down.'[12]

The story of Father Damien, working among the lepers on the Island of Molokai has perhaps been used by preachers so often that it has lost its impact. Imagination is all the more necessary. I once heard a preacher take us to that island and question the people there. ' "Why did you come here?" "When I caught leprosy my family drove me out and I had to come here." "Why are you here?" "It is a government decree: I had to come." "And you?" "The villagers were so afraid of catching leprosy they forced me to leave." Suddenly we notice a priest. "Father, you here!" Quietly he answers, "I chose to come." '

Another preacher took us to the church on the island to listen to Father Damien preaching. He always began his sermon, 'Brothers and sisters', until one day his words are different: 'We lepers . . .' Yet another preacher picked up Robert Louis Stevenson's open letter defending Father Damien against a virulent attack by the Revd Charles M Hyde of Honolulu.[13] Introducing biography into a sermon is more than simply giving a summary of the individual's life or recounting an incident from it.

No work of fiction, unless it be Dostoyevsky's *The Brothers Karamazov*, searches out the problem of suffering more devastatingly than Camus's *The Plague*. Every preacher should read it before attempting to preach on the problem, though after reading the book they may well feel that they have nothing effective to say! To open a sermon with the scene where Dr Bernard Rieux and Father Paneloux sit beside a young boy, dying in agony, will certainly make it impossible for the congregation to evade the problem with the pious platitudes that are so often supposed to soothe the relatives of the sufferer.[14] The priest's 'Perhaps we should love what we cannot understand', and Dr Rieux's 'No, Father. I've a very different idea of love. And until my dying day I shall refuse to love a scheme of things in which children are put to torture' set out the contrast between conventional piety and questioning unbelief. It is a contrast that I have never heard presented in any sermon.

Music

The ways in which music can be imaginatively introduced into sermons are less obvious. Although poetry and other literature depend on the sound of words, the listener is largely unconscious of this. It is the meaning which is heard first of all. Only when the overtones are brought out into the light, as in my earlier illustration from Keats' 'The Eve of St Agnes ', does the importance of the sounds become obvious. Music, however, *is* sound. The fact that opera can be appreciated when it is sung in a foreign and unknown language makes this plain. How, then, can sounds be brought within a sermon?

There is a further barrier. Music can repel as well as attract. It is the exceptional person who enjoys equally all kinds of music. Each member of the congregation and each preacher will have their favourite composer or style of music. The demands made upon the preacher are thus the greater. Yet it is possible to entice the hearers, so that they discover the message despite their initial distaste for the dish that is being offered.

Learning from Bach

Bach's organ music is hardly the kind of music which will be heard in a high street boutique. Yet the composer who declared that so many tunes came to him during the night that he had to be careful not to tread on them when he got up has much to offer.

The two chorale preludes in the *Little Organ Book,* set in opposition, and perhaps played at the beginning and in the middle of a New Year sermon can enable the preacher to draw out the sense of sadness that yet another year has passed and can never be recalled, with all the implications that this has for our lives that slip so quickly by, and then to contrast this with the joy that comes as we look into the future, with all the new opportunities that stretch before us. In *Das alte Jahr vergangen ist* Bach was clearly arrested by the first line: 'The old year now hath passed away', and he overlooked the rest of the verse, which expresses thankfulness for the way God has preserved his people through the year that has ended. The preacher can draw attention to the poignant harmonies, the grief expressed through a chromatic phrase, and the long drawn out arabesque melody. This is sadness incarnate. By contrast, *In dir ist Freude*, with its striking pedal theme that appears no less than 19 times, expresses the joy and hopefulness of the New Year. If we sometimes look forward into the New Year with apprehension and fear, this prelude offers confidence in a God who is 'the true redeemer', as one line of the chorale describes him.

Even greater possibilities are offered through Bach's little prelude for manuals only, *Dies sind die heil'gen zehn Gebot*. How to preach on the Ten Commandments is surely a burden for many of us. Clichés breed clichés. After all, no one is going to object to the commandments. So dull platitudes emerge laboriously from the preacher's lips. This chorale prelude offers a completely novel approach. It is a fugue – 'Oh, how dull,' we exclaim. Then we discover that the fugue is a gigue. Whatever does old Bach think he is playing at? The Ten Commandments as a dance! In fact his prelude tells us a great deal about the Ten Commandments.

In the first place, these are no stern rules to be obeyed with a dour solemnity. There is joy in keeping God's law, as the psalmists knew. 'In the way of thy testimonies I delight as much as in all riches' (Psalm 119:14). The gigue is entirely right.

To understand the riches of Bach's prelude we need to remember that he, as a Lutheran, would have numbered the commandments differently from the way we do. Lutherans and Catholics take the final commands against coveting as two, not one, and combine what we regard as the first two commandments into one.

So back to the prelude. The subject of the fugue is given out in turn by tenor, alto, bass and soprano. Musically this is the exposition: theologically it marks the foundation of the Ten Commandments. There are to be no other gods and no images; God's name is not to be taken lightly, the Sabbath is to be maintained, and father and mother are to be honoured. Expressed differently, the ground on which the religious person's life is built is trust in the one God, absolute truthfulness, a pattern of activity and pauses to worship God and delight in him, and respect within the family.

Then Bach introduces the subject of the fugue four more times, but now inverted. In this way he marks off the next four commandments: you shall not kill, you shall not commit adultery, you shall not steal, you shall not bear false witness. Here is the basis of a healthy and safe society, the kind of society we long for.

Before he allows us to hear the subject again, Bach has a long episode, based on scraps of the tune. In some ways it is the jolliest part of this jolly fugue. What is he up to? Is he giving us time to ponder those first eight commandments? Or is he suggesting that the commandments are to be woven into everyday life – to be there even when we are not immediately conscious of them or only pay them a passing glance? Or has he simply been overcome by joy?

So we come finally to the last two entries of the subject – the two commandments against coveting. By giving them to the bass and soprano, it is as if Bach is stressing the importance of these last two commandments for the whole of Christian living. In this prelude the music is the sermon, and the preacher's words are simply there to enable the congregation to hear it.

Many other examples might be drawn from Bach's astonishing repertoire. It has been suggested, for example, that in another of his preludes on this same chorale Bach is attempting to depict the moral disorder of the world within which the canon on the chorale melody stands for the law. The prelude makes more demands upon the congregation, but the contrast between the trio and the chorale melody could be presented to considerable effect by an imaginative preacher and a competent organist.[15]

Other composers

Preachers who know other composers better than I do will be able to introduce their own favourite musical works in similar ways. Among more recent classical composers, Messiaen's religious mysticism offers many opportunities. Simply to play or listen to some of his more approachable pieces can awaken a sense of goodness that a multitude of worn-out words will certainly fail to achieve.

This last observation indicates that music need not always teach. While many preachers, and I would certainly count myself among them, firmly reject the use of music to work up the congregation into an emotional state which can then be interpreted as religious experience, emotion is a part of human life which we neglect to our peril. If our most important experiences are too deep for words, music – equally with silence – can make room for individuals within the congregation to attain a sense of God. A carefully chosen extract can lead into the sermon or follow it, setting the mood or reinforcing the message. Many of us who are older will remember, from the time when radio was 'the wireless', the inspired choice of Ravel's *Introduction and Allegro* as the theme music for Dorothy Sayers' play cycle *The Man Born to be King*.

To replace the turgid flow of lifeless words, rerun clichés and wilting platitudes, the preacher might consider offering musical settings of biblical texts. John Sawyer has a chapter on Isaiah in literature and music.[16] He observes that the first two parts of Handel's *Messiah* are made up almost entirely of quotations from this prophet. In *Elijah*

Mendelssohn uses Isaiah texts to express his own faith and his Christian interpretation of Elijah. Brahms' *Ein Deutsches Requiem* contains settings of four texts from Isaiah, in Luther's German. Bob Dylan described his *John Wesley Harding* as 'the first biblical rock album'.

In one of his sermons preached in Gray's Inn Chapel, Eric James points out how many musicians have been inspired by the parable of the Prodigal Son: Benjamin Britten's third 'church parable', a cantata by Debussy, a Prokofiev ballet and others.[17]

Music offers a great wealth of possibilities – introduced into the service with a delicate and discerning imagination.

9

LANGUAGE

Words

Words are the preacher's tools, yet it is strange how rarely preachers take time to sharpen them. This may be because they think of the sermon as but a creature of the moment, having a bare 20 minutes' life-span, each word dying as soon as it is uttered. Moreover the age of grand oratory is past, killed by the television which makes every speech a casual conversation. Yet the choice of words still matters. As well as the dictionary meaning, words carry overtones, collected like moss during many years of usage, and these overtones have become part of the meaning that the hearer absorbs. Words are also sounds, which, even if they do not change the strict meaning, make that meaning more accessible.

A rather extreme example will reveal this. One of the most sensuous verses in the English language was written by Keats in 'The Eve of St Agnes'.[1] It begins:

> Full on this casement shone the wintry moon,
> And threw warm gules on Madeline's fair breast.

Madeline is a rather exotic name; let us call her Jane. And then let us express the sense in matter-of-fact words, using prose instead of the rhythm of poetry:

> That January night the full moon shone through the coloured glass of the window and made red marks on Jane's white chest.

Nothing has been lost of the meaning. It is exactly what happened. The moon is shining. We need to mention the stained glass because, in the previous verse, Keats described the casement window in which 'a shielded scutcheon blush'd with blood of queens and kings'. Gules is no more than the heraldic name for red. But you are hardly likely to read my version twice, still less think it has any value.

Words are the preacher's tools, and words matter. Much of the dullness of modern sermons is due to the dreary words, the tired phrases, the standard epithets, and the banal clichés that preachers are content to dole out to their long-suffering congregations.

Coleridge once defined poetry as 'the best words in the best order'. In a letter to Leo Baker, C S Lewis declared this bad as a definition of poetry, since it could apply equally to prose, or indeed to any piece of writing that fulfilled its purpose. 'Thus "The train will leave at 7.30" gives us the best words (for the purpose), in the best order, i.e. we cannot improve upon them. Wordsworth indeed might have written: "The hissing locomotive with her line/ Of labouring coaches from the platform side/ Shall take departure ere the moving index/ On that high, grim chronometer etc.": but this wd. be worse words in a worse order.'[2] Coleridge's definition, however, taken with Lewis' modification, is true of sermons. Preachers should attempt to produce the best words in the best order to fit the purpose of their sermon.

How, then, are they to achieve this? We may recall Francis Bacon's aphorism: 'Reading maketh a full man; conference (conversation) a ready man; and writing an exact man.'[3] Novels are to be enjoyed. Poetry is to delight in. Neither should be read for purely instrumental purposes. But both can instruct and assist the preacher. Reading them does not just offer preachers apt quotations (provided they are stored in a filing system – which most of us are too lazy to do) but also attunes their minds to elegant and effective English. Conversation not only stimulates the mind to be quick to respond to ideas and to set one's thoughts in order, but importantly reveals the difference between spoken and written English. Writing should lead the preacher to select exactly the right word and frame the telling phrase – provided that what the preacher writes is *spoken* English. The distinction is important, but both are vital. Spoken English can all too readily become sloppy, repetitive, cliché-ridden. Written English uses longer sentences (and longer words!). Short sentences and clear progression of thought are essential in the spoken word if the hearer is to understand. The sound of the words is more important: so say the words as you write them, but write before you speak.

A television advert by the Royal Mail reminds us that you cannot reread a telephone call. This attempt to entice the viewers to write letters reminds preachers that their congregations hear their words only once (and not that, if preachers fail to enunciate their words clearly and drop their voice at the end of a sentence). It also draws the preachers' attention to the fact, often forgotten or not realised at all, that their words are heard one at a time, in sequence. They must, therefore, be readily and quickly understood. The progress of the thought must be immediately obvious. Structure matters. It is the developed imagination which will lead the preacher to fasten upon the unusual phase and unexpected word that will capture and retain the attention of the congregation and prevent the sermon from being dull. The imagination must be allowed to range wildly as the preacher thinks out his or her sermon, but it must be a controlled imagination which speaks within the sermon as the preacher delivers it. The imaginative preacher will not be afraid to work on his or her sermon and throw away those 'brilliant' ideas and phrases which do not advance the argument or fit into the structure. A good sermon is a work of art, and the good preacher will expend as much effort on it as the poet, who revises and revises until the poem exactly expresses his inmost thoughts and feelings.

Metaphor and other figures of speech

One feature of language which belongs especially to the sphere of the imagination is metaphor, simile and other figures of speech. The preacher should never undervalue them, for they are the red corpuscles in the lifeblood of oratory and the nerves which allow thought to be conveyed from the brain to the lips and on to the hearers. G B Caird points out that 'comparison is one of our most valuable sources of knowledge, the main road leading from the known to the unknown. . . . God speaks to man in similitudes.' The Hebrew writers were as profligate with metaphors, and mixed metaphors at that, as Shakespeare. R H Kennett commented on Isaiah 28:18 ('When the overflowing scourge sweeps by, you shall be trampled underfoot') that 'a Hebrew sucked the juice out of each metaphor as he used it, and threw away the skin at once'.[4]

Metaphor enables us to see things in new ways. When the poet speaks of 'that little hunchback in the snow' we feel that we have never looked at a robin properly before.[5]

Because the Bible abounds with metaphor, the preacher should be more aware than most of its importance. Sadly, however, one of the grim idiosyncrasies of modern translations is that the translators seem unable to credit today's readers with the ability to understand them, and with a cruel and wanton vandalism they crush them into a smooth prosaic greyness. The *Good News Bible* renders (one might almost say, rends) the metaphors in Isaiah 28 that I have just quoted by: 'When disaster sweeps down, you will be overcome.' Equally crass is its shredding of Isaiah 33:11. Who would guess that the Hebrew that lies beneath 'You make worthless plans and everything you do is useless' is 'You shall conceive chaff and bring forth stubble'? When the psalmist declares: 'Thou knowest when I sit down and when I rise up; . . . Thou searchest out my path and my lying down, and art acquainted with all my ways' *Good News Bible* offers us: 'You know everything I do; . . . You see me, whether I am working or resting; you know all my actions.' God tells the boy Samuel: 'I am about to do a thing in Israel, at which the two ears of every one that hears it will tingle', which GNB flattens to: 'I am going to do something to the people of Israel that is so terrible that everyone who hears it will be stunned' – vigorous, but the metaphor is lost. The familiar words of Jesus, 'Do not let your left hand know what your right hand is doing', express his call not to make a parade of giving alms, but the modern translator, timidly afraid that the readers will take the words literally, offers instead: 'When you help a needy person, do it in such a way that even your closest friend will not know about it.'

This is most disastrous when the metaphors relating to God are turned into commonplace descriptions. In Psalm 144:2 'my rock and my fortress, my stronghold and my deliverer, my shield and he in whom I take refuge' becomes 'He is my protector and defender, my shelter and saviour, in whom I trust for safety.' The Israelite's affirmation: 'The LORD brought us out of Egypt with a mighty hand and an outstretched arm' (Deuteronomy 26:9) is flattened into: 'By his great power and strength he rescued us from Egypt.' As the metaphors are erased the uncontrollable is domesticated, the mystery vanishes, and with it departs the ability to awaken the spirit to the glories of the splendour of God.

Given the wealth of metaphors in the scriptures it is strange that they are found so rarely in sermons. It is as if the preachers were in league with some of the modern versions of the Bible in deliberately flattening the rugged mountainous landscape of the scriptures to a level plain of mediocrity. The preacher should cultivate metaphors, for they lead into hidden pathways and offer the vision of expansive vistas.

'To make you see'

Joseph Conrad, in the Preface to *The Nigger of the Narcissus,* set out his task as 'by the power of the written word, to make you hear, to make you feel – it is, before all, to make you *see*'.[6] In this statement he is exploiting the double sense of 'see' – to 'visualise' and to 'comprehend' or 'gain insight'. Perhaps it is by way of the first that he achieves the second, although it requires the whole novel to see in the second sense. Certainly his novels are teeming with examples of words which bring the scene vividly before us. Consider how a pair of words immediately sets the picture before the reader. Marlow is sitting in his rented seaman's room, sparsely furnished with four-poster bed and mosquito net, chair and table, with Jim standing aloof, tense, at war with himself. It is dark outside and the room is lit by a solitary candle: 'It was very quiet in the room, whose shadows *huddled together* in corners, away from the still flame of the candle flaring upright in the shape of a dagger.'[7]

The task of the preacher is to enable the congregation to *see*, to obtain a fresh vision of goodness, truth, beauty and God. Conrad managed to achieve his aim when writing in what was to him his third language. Surely preachers should be able to do the same in their mother tongue. Congregations will be immensely grateful to those who make the effort to enable them to see the glory of God through the words they use.

In one of my churches when I was a very young minister there were two preachers who had the gift of language and were not afraid to use it. One of them described dull, monotonous speech as 'buzz, buzz, buzz, like a bee in a bottle' and spoke of someone 'looking as miserable as if he had had a coil of barbed wire dragged through him'. The other spoke of walking down the lane in the early morning, the banks and hedgerows heavy with dew, with every blade of grass wearing a diamond ring.

When that prince of preachers, A J Gossip, talked about the prayer of adoration, he took the title of his chapter from Sir Thomas Browne: 'Thinking Magnificently about God'. In it he complained that 'many of us who do seek to give God a place in our lives, seem . . . to have belittled Him to ourselves in our own minds, till we are almost casual in our approaches to Him. . . . We turn into His presence almost nonchalantly, shoving the door open with a lazy shoulder',[8] and by that metaphor made the enormity of our failure vivid in a way that direct statements could never do.

Help in finding the right language

Where can the preacher obtain help in finding the right language? Many find Roget's *Thesaurus* invaluable. Others use the thesaurus supplied by their word-processor program. I myself rely heavily on *Chambers Dictionary of Synonyms and Antonyms*[9] (I have turned to it many times in writing this book to find exactly the right word for a particular place, for synonyms are not identical in meaning, and the overtones add vibrating colour to every word. We would not be likely to speak of the Holy Spirit as 'heavenly pigeon', and few of us would fancy 'dove pie'). While it may now seem old-fashioned, Quiller-Couch's *The Art of Writing*[10] can still help the preacher to avoid the worst clichés and other faults, as well as providing entertaining reading.

Commentaries should be consulted not just to learn about the meaning of the text, but also because from time to time they produce the spark which ignites the imagination. Morna Hooker, discussing that mysterious last chapter of Mark's Gospel, describes the message delivered to the women who fail to pass it on and the promise to the disciples which is left hanging in the air as 'two pieces of non-evidence'.[11] Now *there* is something for imagination to play with. In his *Twelve Months of Sundays,* N T Wright begins one of his reflections on the readings: 'The prince of peace comes with a sword. To that theological oxymoron we must add the sad, and still tragic, story of Abraham, Hagar and Ishmael', and continues: 'Go down into the Genesis story, down the dark staircases of imagination, and even then you will perhaps never plumb the depths of Hagar's misery, of Abraham's dilemma, of Sarah's memories, of Ishmael's destiny.'[12] Most of all, the reading of non-theological books – novels, plays, poetry, biography and well-written history – can give most help in awakening a dormant imagination and feeding a feeble one.

The frenzied imagination

I end this account of language with a warning. Many years ago the principal of my college spoke to us about a book of prayers, and read some words from one of them, and then, with that slight sniff of his that indicated dissent, he commented: 'a bit precious'. The quest for striking expressions and impressive language can easily lead to phrases of which we may be proud but which are very likely to make some members of the congregation cringe. It is a frenzied imagination that seeks for effect. Some feminist writing and preaching suffers badly from it, and the current trend in biblical studies towards literary approaches to the text – rhetorical criticism, reader-response criticism, and the like – fosters it. The dividing line between the precious and the striking is fine indeed, and what is impressive to one hearer is artificial to another. In the end it is a straining imagination which is more likely to err than one which wanders freely and lightly, with a butterfly touch. Preachers need to cultivate the imagination. They must avoid forcing it.

10

BEGINNINGS AND ENDINGS

Beginnings

Beginnings matter. The first sentence of the sermon will either capture the interest of the congregation or make them wonder whether it is worth their while paying any great attention to what the preacher has to say.

The preacher who begins his sermon on Trinity Sunday, 'The last time I preached on the Trinity, a minister in the congregation told me I had preached heresy', is more likely to be listened to than the one who starts off: 'This morning I am going to expound the doctrine of the triune God in whom Christians believe.' Perhaps the preacher who is even bolder and begins: 'Most Christians believe in three Gods. Does it matter?' is even more certain of an attentive hearing.

A quotation may provide the arch through which we may enter the garden of the sermon. An unknown schoolgirl wrote:[1]

> Everyone dies
> Like an amateur,
> For they know
> No other way.

Even those preachers who have allowed their imaginations to shrivel must surely find here many ideas for developing a sermon on death, while few in a congregation will be able to turn aside from these evocative words. Even so care needs to be taken with the way we introduce them. A bare quotation? Perhaps. 'Everyone dies' is a truism which forces the congregation to wonder what the preacher will say next, and 'Like an amateur' comes with a considerable shock. So we might start off with the quotation without any preliminary explanation. Or the preacher may prefer a more gentle approach: 'I do not know her name. I do not know when she was born, or where. I do not know what became of her. I only know that she wrote a four-line poem that a friend of mine chanced upon in a school magazine.'

If we wish to enable the congregation to understand what a strange land the Bible is, a novel beginning might be to quote a slogan or an instruction of 50 or more years ago, the meaning of which will elude most of them. I used to quote, 'Be like Dad, keep Mum', to my students. They understood every word individually, of course, and could fit the nouns and verbs together, but they did not have the least idea what it meant. Even when I added another slogan from the time of the Second World War, 'Careless talk costs lives', they did not grasp what it was all about. Still more enigmatic was the direction, 'Pull frog for curve'. You needed to have lived at the time of trolley buses, and been at the junction when the conductor forgot to pull the handle on the post supporting the trolley wires and you could watch the arms of the trolley bus fly up into the air as the driver went one way and the arms tried to go another. Then you would know that the 'frog' was the 'points'. If it is so difficult to know what a slogan and an instruction from a mere 60 years ago means, there is no wonder that we often find it difficult to grasp the meaning of some of the sayings of the prophets or the words of the psalmist! I have used this ploy to open a sermon on Hosea 6:1-6, but it obviously has much wider possibilities.

I have mentioned Robert Davidson already in this book. Alastair G Hunter tells us in his contribution to a book of essays in Davidson's honour that the greatly loved Professor once preached a sermon which began with the words: '"I see that the Young Master has returned," said the Fatted Calf'.[2] It is a brilliant opening, by a preacher who knew how to look at things with imagination.

I once began a sermon: 'Mary had a little lamb, with roast potatoes, Brussels sprouts and mint sauce', and pointed out that the meaning was not apparent until I had reached the end of the sentence. It was only then that the hearers realised that I had been leading them up the garden path. They had taken the first five words in the familiar way, and then had had to shift from the nursery to the restaurant. They had even given the wrong sense to the verb. And the lamb was not a lively woolly animal, skipping behind Mary, but a few slices carved from a leg or a shoulder. I used it to introduce a sermon on old age. In it I suggested that we understand the meaning of our lives only when we have come near their end. Only then can we remember all the things that seemed at the time no more than chance but now can be seen to have led us to where we now are as if by some deliberate purpose. I went on to suggest that we should look back with thanksgiving, gratitude, and sometimes regret and shame, and should accept the limitations that come with old age, as Barzillai did (2 Samuel 19:34-37). But the sentence could equally have been the opening of a sermon on eschatology.

Derrick Greeves stated in the first sentence of a Harvest Festival sermon: 'You will understand the significance of Harvest Festival if your house has ever been burgled.'[3] What he meant is not obvious – and that is what makes it an excellent beginning. (He went on to say: 'You will have felt a sense of righteous indignation, that anyone should have the effrontery to come onto your premises, make themselves at home, even dare to use your facilities, and take away your property as their own right.' And then: 'The point about Harvest Festival . . . is that from time to time we pull ourselves together and remember where we are. We are living on someone's property and someone's charity. "The earth is the Lord's and all that is in it." ')

Many years ago I heard D W Cleverley Ford say in a lecture: 'If I met Jesus I am not sure that I would like him.' Few congregations could fail to be attentive to the preacher who began his sermon with that sentence.

So it is worth the preacher's while spending quite a lot of time allowing his or her imagination to roam freely and then to chisel the first three sentences until they are so sculpted that they will capture the attention of the congregation. After that, it is up to the preacher to maintain the interest!

Naturally those first three sentences will relate to what is to follow, but imagination is often wayward – that is its charm – and how they relate may not be immediately clear. The poet tells us that truth stands on a huge hill and those who would find her must wind round and round again in order to reach her.[4] An incident, a quotation, a statement that seems far removed from the biblical passage may be the way to entice the congregation to discover its central meaning.

Yet we must control the imagination. Colin Gunton began one of his sermons with these sentences:[5]

> 'How should we speak to children we know to be dying?' asked the writer of an article in *The Independent* the other day. Do we tell them they are going to get better, when we know that almost certainly they are not? Would that not be false comfort, often recognised as such by its object? Do we tell them that they are going to heaven? That is more difficult. As the writer commented, his wife believes in heaven, but he thinks that he does not. Suppose they were faced with such a situation, what would they do? What is true and what is false comfort?

The sermon was preached on the Fourth Sunday in Advent, 1996, and a fine sermon it is on Matthew 1:18-25, Matthew's use of Isaiah 7:14, and the incarnation. The theme of true and false comfort runs through it. But is not the opening too strong for the purpose it serves? Will not some in the congregation want an answer to the question that the writer in *The Independent* raised, and go on thinking about it during the whole of the rest of the sermon? Might there not even be someone in the congregation who is facing or has faced just that cruel dilemma?

Endings

When the preacher comes to the end of the sermon he or she should stop – even if its suddenness causes the organist to scramble to the organ stool and frantically switch on the blower for the next hymn. Far better an abrupt close than a procession of weary sentences that meander across the long-suffering pews.

Yet endings are as important as beginnings. What is to be avoided absolutely and without any exception is to labour the moral (as I have already pointed out). Preachers simply will not credit children or adults with sufficient intelligence to see what they are driving at. Jesus never made this mistake. The 'explanations' of several of his parables are so different from the parables themselves that we must surely suppose they come from later followers who, like anxious preachers, did not believe that the parable could convey its message without their meddling.

So how do we end the sermon?

Michael Townsend once pointed out[6] that a sermon on 'The Christian Attitude to Death' could end: 'To die is, as we are taught by our faith, to pass to that realm where we await our share in the resurrection. Because of the death and resurrection of Jesus Christ we have been promised that the power of death has been broken and the final victory belongs not with death, the last enemy, but with God who will give us new and risen life.' Or it could end with a quotation from the tenth of John Donne's *Holy Sonnets*:

One short sleep past, we wake eternally,
And death shall be no more; death thou shalt die.

Either way, this ends the sermon with a note of triumph, possibly more defiantly in the Donne quotation. But what if our faith is less secure and we wish to be honest with our congregation?

I once wrote a sermon on Luke 20:27-38, to which I gave the title 'Bleak Confidence'. In it I contrasted Jesus' certainty that there is a life after death with his declaration that in heaven the dead will be like the angels and will not marry. I pointed out that for many of us our marriage is the most wonderful thing that ever happened to us – and Jesus says it will be lost in the world after death! So I ended the sermon: 'In this story in the gospel there is firm confidence, absolute certainty in life after death, but also a rather bleak picture. "He is not God of the dead, but of the living": "they neither marry nor are given in marriage." We can only hope that heaven will be better than we suppose.'

There is more to this, however, than simply finding a memorable ending. The way the sermon ends will depend on the aim which the preacher has for the sermon. A sermon which seeks to lift the congregation into the presence of the incomprehensible God will end with words that evoke a sense of wonder and awe. A sermon which explores spiritual or intellectual difficulties may end either in quiet confidence or with a sentence that leaves the way open for further thought. A sermon which sets out the Christian gospel may possibly end with a call to accept the offer, though the preacher should be sensitive to what is appropriate within the particular service and for the actual congregation that is present. Jesus often ended his parables with a question or simply left it to his hearers to draw their own conclusions. It is something that preachers are all too seldom willing to do.

11

GETTING THE SERMON PAST THE PEN

The Mellstock choir tried to put their finger on what it was that prevented their new vicar from being a 'spouter', as Mr Penny, the shoemaker, put it. All they could come up with was that 'he hadn't been able to get it past his pen'.[1]

It is a fault which is difficult to describe, but of which every congregation is aware, even if they are as much at a loss to say precisely what is wrong as the members of the Mellstock choir. They sense that the sermon lacks life. I do not mean liveliness. The theme may be serious and a solemn style called for. No. What is wrong is that it is stodgy. What the preacher says may well be sound. The problem is that his or her ideas are dressed in the wrong clothes. It is on the occasions when this happens that, as I sit on the organ stool and listen to the preacher, I most want to jump up and say: 'You have wrecked that. The thought was excellent, but you have managed to make the splendour of the divine majesty sound as if it were the report of an official government enquiry. Have you no imagination?'

I am not sure that I can illustrate what I am getting at, but I regard it as so important that I must try.

Matthew 2:13-23 (Year A. Christmas 1)

The gospel is Matthew 2:13-23. With diligence our hypothetical *preacher*[2] has turned to the commentaries. The commentator she chances upon[3] points out that this is the final section of Matthew's birth and infancy stories, its language is highly Matthaean, and Matthaean also are the themes running through the passage: the wickedness of a Jewish king and the providence and intervention of God. The commentator refers to the story as 'legend'. He points out that threats to the life of a saviour soon after birth were almost universal in the ancient world, and compares Moses. Matthew believes that Jesus was God's Son, miraculously conceived and destined to the highest office under God: he will judge the world on the last day. The exact details of his life had been prophesied by God through the prophets. Moreover Matthew's readers were probably the victims of persecution. The commentator draws attention to the contrast between Matthew's world and ours. Matthew was a first-century Jewish teacher who had become a follower of Jesus and holds office in a church largely composed of Jewish converts. Yet even today it is necessary for Christians who believe in a good and loving providence to try to make some sense of the fact of evil and the tragedies that happen to 'holy innocents'.

It is not terribly promising. But the *preacher* makes a serious attempt to incorporate the ideas of the commentator into her sermon. She begins:

> *Each of the evangelists begins his gospel in a different way. This year we are following Matthew. He was a Jewish teacher before he became a Christian and he is interested in the way the Old Testament prophets foretold the birth and the life of Jesus. You may have noticed how many texts Matthew quotes. Matthew also finds parallels in the story of Moses. Like Moses, an evil king tried to kill him soon after he was born. Pharaoh made a law that every Jewish boy should be put to death. Herod, when he found that the wise men had gone home without telling him where the baby prince could be found, struck out wildly, and to make sure that the rival 'king' had not been*

missed out, he put to death all the boys up to two years old. But God had already planned Jesus' escape. He warned Joseph in a dream and the holy family fled to Egypt.

The *preacher* then explained that what Herod did was entirely in keeping with his character, and gave illustrations of the way he had executed everyone he thought was plotting against him or who might be a threat to him, in the end killing almost all his family, including his beloved wife Mariamme. This led into a confident assertion that God protects his children, and developed into an account of providence.

This is a worthy *preacher* who has tried to deal honestly with the text, and what she said could not fail to be of value to those who were still listening. It would certainly not fall under the wry comment of George Herbert, who, after warning us not to judge the preacher, 'for he is thy Judge', adds:

> The worst speak something good: if all want sense
> God takes a text, and preacheth patience.[4]

'Each of the evangelists begins his gospel in a different way' is not an utterly impossible way to start. Probably few in the congregation will have thought of it. Yet it is a little remote, and the distance between *preacher* and congregation widens as she proceeds. Let us try to make a fresh start.

> Do we have to return to the real world so soon after Christmas? The candles are extinguished. Those who have jobs will soon be back to work. Those who sleep rough will drift back to the railway arches or their cardboard cities after their brief encounters with charity and a warm bed. The fighting continues in Israel. The mothers and children in Africa go on dying – as they have been dying all over Christmas. Those governments which Amnesty International has condemned for torturing their own citizens resume their barbarisms. We may

> wish to stay a little longer in the season of joy and peace, but the gospel which we have just read takes us back to this 'real' world.

That's better. The first sentence reflects the mood of many in the congregation. The evils that are listed both echo the reading and arouse the demand for an answer to the question, Why? The scene is set to draw the contrast between the festival of goodwill and the life that many people have to endure.

The preacher might go on:

> The gospel continues the story of the wise men, whom the children portrayed in their nativity play. But this incident was not in that play. It is too harsh for children – or for us as we celebrate Christmas. Mary, Joseph and Jesus escape to Egypt. Herod orders the murder of all the boys in Bethlehem who are under two years old. There is no evidence that it ever happened. Matthew may have created the story in order to weave in a couple of biblical texts and a quotation that has never been traced. He believed that everything that happened to Jesus had been foretold by the prophets. Yet it is true to life. That is what Herod was like. Insanely jealous. Neurotically afraid of enemies. He ended up by having his beloved wife Mariamme executed, and almost his final act was to order the death of one of his sons.
>
> The gospel holds before us the world as it was, and forces us to turn our gaze on the world as it is today. We do not even need to go outside our own country. A young mother is murdered and her little boy beaten up as they walk on Wimbledon Common. Two Chinese students are assaulted by a gang of white youths as they quietly walk home. An man in his 90s is seriously injured by an intruder because he had no money in the house. We have grown accustomed to armour-plated security vans delivering or collecting cash. It isn't safe for doctors

to visit patients in the middle of the night. In hospitals a nurse's uniform is no longer sacrosanct.

Yet Matthew did not write this story in order to set out this dark picture of the world. He tells of an angel appearing to Joseph in a dream and warning him of the danger, and of a child and his parents who escaped the massacre. God protected his son.

But what of the other boys in Bethlehem? Their mothers could not join in the thanksgiving. We may hope that Matthew did indeed make up the story and that it is not true that God saved one boy while allowing all the others to die.

The preacher has now brought the gospel reading round to the problem which she wishes to discuss. Everything will depend on how that discussion is carried on.

But this is not the only way to begin. A harsher start, if the sermon followed immediately on the gospel reading, might be to say:

> No angel of the Lord appeared in a dream to the mothers of those other boys in Bethlehem. God just let them die. All he did was to protect his son.

Romans 14:1-12 (Year A. Proper 19)

The *preacher* has obviously read the commentaries, or one of the volumes of notes on the Lectionary readings, and begins his sermon:

> *In the reading we have just listened to, Paul addresses some specific quarrels among the Christians in Rome, and articulates a theological framework for dealing with them. The quarrels have to do with diet and observing special days, probably the Sabbath. Some members of the church are vegetarians, others are prepared to eat meat, even if it is non-kosher or has been dedicated to a pagan god. The problems seem remote from our world. Some of you are probably vegetarians, but you do not regard it as a*

religious matter, and although we had the 'Keep Sunday Special' campaign, it didn't split the church. Yet Christians are sharply divided about such things as abortion, homosexuality, women priests, and even the types of hymns we sing. So what Paul said to the Christians in Rome may be helpful to us as well.

The *preacher* went on to state that Paul's response was not to side with either party in the church, but to say that what is important is that each person has thought out their position and that their conscience is clear. The health of the community is to take precedence over 'right' belief or 'right' conduct. He ended the sermon:

It might appear that Paul is advocating a complete individualism. Believers belong to God and are accountable only to God and not to one another. So they must act according to their own consciences and convictions. This is not so. He places this individualism within a community context. What he seeks is not a tolerance of diversity, or a grudging acceptance of the inevitability of differences of opinion. Instead he calls for an active welcoming of those with conflicting views and practices. Christ welcomed everyone, and Christians must do the same.

It is all very sound and is expressed clearly enough. The *preacher* has tried to relate it to the present day and any congregation would benefit from it. The trouble is that by clinging so closely to what the commentator says – even to the extent of reproducing 'commentary' language – the sermon never reaches the hearts of the congregation. Here is a worthy preacher, but not a very imaginative one.

So what can be done to brighten it up?

In the first place it will not do to begin as the *preacher* did. If a preacher wishes to keep closely to the reading, the sermon might have begun:

Come with me to Rome in Paul's day. The church is in uproar. Some of the members believe that Christians should avoid eating meat. All the meat in

> the butchers' shops had been offered to pagan gods before it was put on sale. The Jews were able to get kosher meat, but that was for Jews only. So these church members said it was best not to eat meat at all. Other church members scoffed at the idea: 'We are Christians, not Jews', they say. 'Christ freed us from keeping the Jewish Law. And how can dedicating the ox to a god who doesn't exist affect the meat? God created all the animals, and so they are good for food. You are only semi-Christians.' The others retort, 'And you are not real Christians at all.'

That's better. But perhaps it is still a bit remote from the congregation. Perhaps the preacher should take an imaginative plunge.

> It was 1948. The two old people had moved into an almshouse, and they invited a young couple and myself to tea to see it. It was a lovely little house – cosy and warm, and just right for them. They were obviously delighted with it. Then we sat down to tea. 'Would you say grace for us?' the old man asked. There was an embarrassing silence. Then the young wife said: 'We don't say grace at home, and I don't think it would be right to say grace now.' The gracious old lady came in quickly to rescue the situation. 'Father always says grace.' And then turning to him, she said: 'Say it to yourself, dear.'
>
> It was only a little incident, but it made me realise how important quite small differences can be to many people in church. Times have changed, and probably very few of us here say grace before meals. But there are other things that divide us – abortion, euthanasia, homosexuality, women priests, whether to baptise babies, even the kind of hymns we should sing. Has what Paul said to the Christians in Rome anything to say to us?

This has the advantage of taking a practice which now sounds a bit old-fashioned. It makes it possible for the congregation to realise that there is a gap between Paul and ourselves, as there is between the old couple of 50 years ago and today.

The more adventurous preacher might even take an issue which is actually dividing the congregation. This, however, is very tricky, and only a preacher who is trusted by the congregation could attempt it directly. It might be possible, however, to approach it with an invented situation.

> Come with me to St Michael's. Jackie and Peter run the youth club. Everyone in the church agrees that they are making a splendid job of it. They have a knack of getting on the young people's wavelength. The church is growing because of the club. Peter even made contact with a delinquent gang, and although most of them don't come to the youth club regularly, they now have a different idea of the Church and of ministers.
>
> Then the rumours started. Peter was spending the night in Jackie's flat. One of the more outspoken church members challenged him outright. He laughed. 'That's right,' he said. 'In fact next week I'm moving in permanently.' It split the church. There were some who said that Jackie and Peter should no longer be allowed to run the youth club. It would set a bad example to the young people and give the church a bad name. Others said that we have to move with the times. Jackie and Peter were only doing what most young people did. They were serious, and had entered into a 'stable relationship'. And after all, wasn't it up to them?
>
> Both sides appealed to the minister. What should she do?

Both of these last two openings would lead into an account of Paul and the church in Rome. The preacher would be able to show that, although the issues were different, the way that Paul dealt with them can help us deal with differences of opinion that can split the church today.

What of the *preacher's* ending? The final sentence exactly sets out the message of the text and is splendid. But the rest of the paragraph limps along on abstract nouns: 'community context', 'tolerance of diversity', 'grudging acceptance', 'inevitability of differences of opinion', 'active welcoming', 'conflicting views'. Every preacher should remember that verbs are alive, concrete nouns are strong and vivid, but abstract nouns drift into a mist. So we might suggest:

> Does this mean that what makes anything right is that we do it with a clear conscience? Are we to accept that everyone is different? All have different ideas of what is right, and they do what their conscience tells them. We ought to be tolerant of other people. So don't criticise Jackie and Peter.
>
> That is not what Paul is saying. His point is this. This man is a vegetarian: that woman eats meat and enjoys it. This woman refuses to shop on Sundays: this man says, 'God made every day, so there is no reason why we shouldn't do the shopping when it is most convenient.' This man holds Christian marriage to be so important that only those who are virgin or married should be members of the Church: that woman says that it is up to the individual to decide how they wish to live. But all are members of the Church. We should be glad that they are. Christ welcomed everyone: we must do the same.

Job 38:1-11 (Year B. Proper 7)

I suggested earlier that one of the aims of the preacher, perhaps the most important aim, is to enable the congregation to obtain a fresh vision of goodness, truth, beauty and God. What passage enables them to achieve this better than the great speeches of God from out of the whirlwind at the end of the book of Job? The Lectionary offers only verses 1-11 (or 1-7 + 34-41) of chapter 38. Here, if ever, is an occasion when the preacher ought boldly to reach out beyond the set verses and preach on the whole speech and Job's response. Few passages present the majesty of the incomprehensible God more magnificently. And few passages present the preacher with a more daunting task – to enable the congregation to encounter the incomprehensible God that the poet of long ago glimpsed. How might it be done?

One set of notes on the Lectionary readings shows with crass crudity what must *not* be offered:[5]

> The Track 2 reading from Job is the beginning of God's response to Job after all his complaints. God has given Job a horrible time, and Job's friends have come and 'comforted' him – if that is the right word. Their various observations on his plight boiled down to the view that Job must have earned God's displeasure in some way for all those things to have happened to him which are related in Job 1. Job has maintained his innocence throughout his ordeal and his comforters have not been able to get him to see his 'folly'. Now God himself responds to all that has been said and, in a grossly imbalanced (*sic*) show of strength, asserts his authority over Job, over his friends and, indeed, over all creation. Job had never claimed to have the Creator's control over all things, but now he is judged as if he had made just such a blasphemous claim. Still Job is the object of God's unpleasantness.

That is all those particular notes have to offer! It is not likely to inspire a sermon that will bring the congregation face to face with God. Indeed, it is difficult to see what sermon could be preached from it. So how might an imaginative preacher take up his or her task? Perhaps the sermon might go something like this:

> I wonder whether the writer of the epistle of James had ever read the Book of Job – right through, that is. The AV's 'Ye have heard of the patience of Job' (James 5:11) has given us a proverb. Even if the Greek is perhaps more correctly translated 'steadfastness', 'persever-ance' or 'endurance', it

rather looks as if he didn't get much further than chapter 2. Which is a pity. For most of the book consists of fierce debate – Job's debate with his friends and his debate with his God. He accuses God of being a cruel torturer, who spies on the lives of men and women to catch them out. His words are savage and wild. He has almost proved the Satan right: 'Touch his bone and his flesh and he will curse thee to thy face.' He utters his final challenge. 'Here is my record, God. If you took the trouble to pay attention to it, you would realise how wrong you have been in treating me like this.'

Then God speaks – and Job is faced with the mystery of deity. God brings before him the wonders of nature in question after question:

'Where were you when I laid the foundations
of the earth?
Have the gates of death been revealed to you?
Have you entered the storehouses of the
snow?
Can you bind the chains of the Pleiades, or
loose the cords of Orion?
Do you know when the mountain goats bring
forth?
Is the wild ox willing to serve you?
Is it by your wisdom that the hawk soars?'

And before this mystery Job is humbled. At last he discovers what religion is all about – the heart of religion is mystery, abasement, faith. The incomprehensible God has been revealed to him through the incomprehensibility of nature.

But we live in a world of science and technology. We can answer God's questions.

'Where were you when I laid the foundations of the earth?' We weren't there, but we can give an account of the first millionths of a second when the universe began.

'Have you entered the storehouses of the snow?' We can predict sunshine and storm, and watch the moving weather systems by satellite.

'Can you control the calving of the hinds?' We practise artificial insemination and know the DNA code and can modify the genes.

'Can you draw out Leviathan with a fishhook?' No, but we could easily construct a mechanical grab to haul him out.

We know all mysteries and all knowledge – well, almost – and to remove mountains we do not need faith any more but only our earth-moving machinery.

Yet the heart of religion remains mystery, abasement, faith – awe before the fascinating and fearful God, the God who is incomprehensible.

Is religion no longer possible, then? Has it been wounded by science, destroyed by knowledge?

We cannot return to the mystery of religion by shutting our eyes. We cannot put science away. It is all around us. We are no longer able to gaze at the stars with the eyes of the psalmist. Dinosaurs have replaced the animals entering Noah's ark two by two. We know the answers to Job's questions and nature can never be the same again.

In a strange way increasing knowledge increases the mystery. The psalmist looked up at stars shining more brilliantly than we shall ever see them. Our night sky never darkens beyond the twilight that we have created with our earthbound light. Yet science has revealed a universe too immense for the imagination to grasp, stranger than we could ever have conceived.

To the biblical writer the activities of the wild animals were a fascinating riddle: to us the nature programmes on the television take us beneath the sea. We creep into the badger's set. We follow the migration of a swallow. We gaze at bacilli. The way in which the wild creatures evolved is reconstructed before our eyes.

We are amazed at the wonders of the natural world, but with that amazement comes a fearful thought: Is this all there is? Is it just there – a bare fact, stark and barren? When the last human being dies, through the pollution of our planet or the final destruction of the solar system, will there remain only the silence of the electrons? Or is there a spiritual Being behind it?

If glory is to be found it must be here.

For us the way to the sacred mystery is not through the unknown, but through what has been discovered: not through ignorance but through breathtaking knowledge. The astrophysicists are today's true mystics.

Job thought that he could stride into God's presence like a prince, flaunting his credentials. 'Look at my CV,' he declared. But after God had paraded the mysteries of nature before him, he admitted: 'I have uttered what I did not understand.' At last he had grasped what religion truly is. His goodness was real, but it formed an impenetrable mist, blocking the way to God. Now the brilliant sunlight of the divine presence has burnt that mist away. God is revealed and Job is aware of him for the first time. 'I had heard of thee by the hearing of the ear, but now my eye sees thee; therefore I despise myself, and repent in dust and ashes.'

Job discovered the incomprehensible God through the incomprehensibilities of nature. To us nature is no longer incomprehensible. Yet the God who is beyond nature remains the one who is beyond our understanding. For the greater the wonders of nature, the greater is the wonder of God. Then, like Job and all the greatest mystics, with a fearful tremor of faith we fall on our faces before the likeness of the appearance of the glory of God.[6]

12

THE BEST FOR GOD

In our garden each year we try to grow that all-too-feeble climbing plant, Morning Glory. The brilliant blue of the flowers is inexpressibly beautiful. But by midday the edges have become ragged: by evening all that remains is a shrivelled twist of petals. 'Even Solomon in all his glory . . .'

Let imagination set this resolve in the preacher's heart: I will make my sermon today as beautiful as the flowers of Morning Glory. I will not be dispirited by the brevity of its life. However small the congregation I expect to be there, I will not skimp the time needed for the imagination to play upon the text. I will let it take me to the strange land of the Bible, and, thrusting my 21st-century prejudices aside, I will seek to understand the thoughts and feelings of the men and women who inhabit the Old Testament and the New. I will not try to force the text into my own ways of thinking, but I will enter into dialogue with it, accepting that it comes from an alien world. When my imagination suggests that I should contradict the text, I will implore it to show me why this should be, and whether what I say will help the congregation to believe or make it more difficult for them to worship. When I preach on one of the great passages, I will summon imagination the more urgently, fearful lest I make holy things common or bring down the majesty of God to the level of the everyday. When I come to write my sermon, I will seek out every word as if I were writing an immortal sonnet. I will craft each sentence with as much care as Gibbon took over the *Decline and Fall*, though never forgetting that it is the spoken word that I am creating. From the moment I first read through the text until I put down my pen, or press the keys to make my computer print out what I have written, I will hold in my mind the words of the old countryman as he picked out the finest apples from his crop for the Harvest Festival: 'Only the very best for God'.[1]

NOTES

Chapter 1

1. Peter Medawar, *Memoir of a Thinking Radish,* OUP, 1986, p.109.

2. Robert Lynd, 'On Poetry and the Modern Man', Introduction to *An Anthology of Modern Verse* compiled by A Methuen, Methuen, 1943 edn., xvi–xix.

3. Quoted by N T Wright, *Twelve Months of Sundays: Reflections on Bible Readings Year A,* SPCK, 2001 p.50.

4. Alastair G Hunter, 'Whose Land Is It Anyway?' in Robert P Carroll and Alastair G Hunter, eds., *Words at Work: Using the Bible in the Academy, the Community and the Churches,* Trinity St Mungo Press, 1994, p.41.

Chapter 2

1. Alister McGrath, *In the Beginning: The Story of the King James Bible,* Hodder & Stoughton, 2001, pp.263-264.

2. Quoted in G B Caird, *The Language and Imagery of the Bible,* Duckworth, 1980, p.145.

3. See K H Strange & R G E Sandbach, compilers, *Psalm 23: An Anthology,* Saint Andrew Press, 1970, revised and extended 1978, new edition 1987.

4. David H C Read, 'The Quality of Eternity', *The Expository Times* 94, 1982–83 p.273.

5. H St J Hart, *A Foreword to the Old Testament,* A & C Black, 1951, pp.177-178.

Chapter 3

1. Gordon Haight, *George Eliot: A Biography,* OUP, 1968, Penguin Books, 1985, pp.145–167, 179.

2. Thomas Hardy, *The Woodlanders,* Penguin Classics, 1986, pp.333–338, 358.

3. Bruce W Winter, *After Paul Left Corinth: The Influence of Secular Ethics and Social Change,* Eerdmans, 2001.

Chapter 4

1. This is frequently quoted in books on Esther. It comes from Luther's *Tischreden.* I take it from Otto Eissfeldt, *The Old Testament: An Introduction,* translated by Peter R Ackroyd, Basil Blackwell, 1975, p.512.

2. We may point to Falk, who had once kept himself alive by resorting to cannibalism – his drawing of his hands down his face is symbolic of the anguish from which he can never escape – Captain Whalley who, going blind, was unable to steer his ship, yet was anxious to complete his term of service to earn money for his daughter, or Lord Jim, who had to come to terms with his desertion of a ship loaded with pilgrims going to Mecca. By narrowing the focus down to one individual Conrad enables us to feel the full impact of the ethical dilemma and the stresses under which his hero is placed.

3. Valuable discussions of the afterlife of biblical texts are to be found in John F A Sawyer, *The Fifth Gospel: Isaiah in the History of Christianity,* CUP, 1996, in which he traces the influence of Isaiah from earliest times until the present, David Brown's two volumes, *Tradition and Imagination,* OUP, 1999, and *Discipleship and Imagination,* OUP, 2000, especially the second, and John Barton's *Oracles of God: Perception of Ancient Prophecy in Israel after the Exile,* Darton, Longman & Todd, 1986.

Chapter 5

1. Trevor Beeson, *Window on Westminster: A Canon's Diary 1976-1987,* SCM, 1998, p.197-198.

2. Hugh Montefiore, *Oh God, What Next?,* Hodder & Stoughton, 1995, pp.1-2.

3. *Jubilees* 17:16. James H. Charlesworth, ed., *The Old Testament Pseudepigrapha,* Volume 2, Darton, Longman & Todd, 1985, p.174.

4. Sebastian Brock, 'Genesis 22: Where was Sarah?, *The Expository Times* 96, 1984–85, p.14–17.

5. The pun can be partially reproduced in English: 'A basket of summer fruit ... A summary end will come ...'

6. N T Wright, *Twelve Months of Sundays: Reflections on Bible Readings Year A,* SPCK, 2001, p.75.

Chapter 6

1. G B Caird, *The Language and Imagery of the Bible,* Duckworth, 1980, p.153.

2. Robert Browning, *The Ring and the Book* (many editions, e.g. Everyman's Library, Dent, 1962).

3. *The Guardian*, Tuesday, 2nd January 2001 (G2, 2-3).

4. Michael Townsend has drawn my attention to an early Christian graffito which depicts the Good Shepherd with a *goat* on his shoulders. This is referred to in Matthew Arnold's poem 'The Good Shepherd with the Kid'.

5. John M Hull, *Touching the Rock: An Experience of Blindness,* SCM, 1990; *In the Beginning There was Darkness,* SCM, 2001.

Chapter 7

1. Robert Davidson, *The Courage to Doubt,* SCM, 1983, pp.97, 98.

2. John Keats, 'Lamia', Pt 2, lines 231-233.

3. Ann Lewin, 'Disclosure', from *Candles and Kingfishers,* in Kathy Keay, compiler, *Laughter, Silence and Shouting,* HarperCollins, 1994, p.172.

4. Rudolf Otto, *The Idea of the Holy: An Inquiry into the non-rational factor in the idea of the divine and its relation to the rational,* translated by John W Harvey, OUP, 1923, 2nd edition, 1950.

5. Thomas Binney, *Hymns & Psalms* 458, *Common Praise* 414, *Rejoice & Sing* 83, *Baptist Praise & Worship* 85.

6. David H C Read, 'The Quality of Eternity', *The Expository Times* 94, 1982-83, p.273.

Chapter 8

1. Charles Williams, 'At the "Ye that do truly"', in Donald Davie, ed., *The New Oxford Book of Christian Verse,* OUP, 1981, p.257.

2. G Ronald Murphy, SJ, *The Heliand: The Saxon Gospel. A Translation and Commentary,* OUP, 1992. See also his *The Saxon Savior: The Germanic Transformation of the Gospel in the Ninth-Century Heliand,* OUP, 1989.

3. See the translation by Helen Gardner in H W Robson, ed., *Essays and Poems Presented to Lord David Cecil,* Constable, 1970, pp.18-36.

4. Robert Henryson, 'The Bludy Serk', in Lord David Cecil, ed., *The Oxford Book of Christian Verse,* OUP, 1940, pp.19–23.

5. G A Studdert-Kennedy, *The Unutterable Beauty,* Hodder & Stoughton, 1927, pp.2, 131.

6. David Gascoyne, 'Ecce Homo', Helen Gardner, ed., *The Faber Book of Religious Verse,* Faber & Faber, 1972, pp.333–335.

7. J A W Bennett, *Poetry of the Passion: Studies in Twelve Centuries of English Verse,* OUP, 1982.

8. Ogden Nash, 'Portrait of the Artist as a Prematurely Old Man', quoted in S Dennis Ford, *Sins of Omission: A Primer on Moral Indifference,* Fortress Press, 1990, p.6.

9. Fred Pratt Green, *The Hymns and Ballads of Fred Pratt Green with Commentary by Bernard Braley,* Hope Publishing Company and Stainer & Bell, 1982, p.20.

10. W E Sangster, *The Craft of Sermon Illustration,* Epworth Press, 1946, reissued in *The Craft of the Sermon,* Epworth Press, 1954.

11. Keith Clements, *Faith on the Frontier: A Life of J H Oldham,* T & T Clark/WCC Publications, 1999, p.465-466.

12. Roy Coad, *Laing: The Biography of Sir John W Laing, CBE, (1879-1978),* Hodder & Stoughton, 1979.

13. Robert Louis Stevenson, *Father Damien: An Open Letter to the Reverend Dr Hyde of Honolulu,* privately printed in Sydney, 1890.

14. Albert Camus, *The Plague,* translated Stuart Gilbert, Penguin, 1947, p.178.

15. See Harvey Grace, *The Organ Works of Bach,* Novello, 1922, esp. pp.114, 122, 137, 213.

16. John F A Sawyer, *The Fifth Gospel: Isaiah in the History of Christianity,* CUP, 1996, pp.158-176, see esp. pp.171-176.

17. Eric James, *Judge Not: A Selection of Sermons Preached in Gray's Inn Chapel 1978–1988*, Christian Action, 1989, p.59.

Chapter 9

1. John Keats, 'The Eve of St Agnes', XXV.

2. C S Lewis, *Collected Letters:* Volume 1. *Family Letters 1905–1931*, edited by Walter Hooper, HarperCollins, 2000, p.508 (letter to Leo Baker, 25th September 1920).

3. Francis Bacon, *Essays* (1625), 'Of Studies', in Angela Partington, ed., *The Oxford Dictionary of Quotations*, 4th Revised Edition, 1996, 44.28.

4. G B Caird, *The Language and Imagery of the Bible*, Duckworth, 1980, p.145; the Kennett quotation (from *In Our Tongues*, 8) is on p.150.

5. Robert Lynd, 'On Poetry and the Modern Man', Introduction to *An Anthology of Modern Verse* compiled by A Methuen, Methuen, 1943 edn., p.xxiii. The poet referred to is W H Davies.

6. Joseph Conrad, *The Nigger of the Narcissus*, Penguin, 1989 (the original was published in 1897, though the title page gave the date as 1898) p.xiix. See also Cedric Watts' note on p.131.

7. Joseph Conrad, *Lord Jim*, Penguin Popular Classics, 1994 (originally published in *Blackwood's Edinburgh Magazine*, 1899-1900), p.141.

8. Arthur John Gossip, *In the Secret Place of the Most High*, Independent Press, 1946, p.118.

9. Martin H Manser, ed., *Chambers Dictionary of Synonyms and Antonyms*, W & R Chambers/CUP, 1989.

10. A T Quiller-Couch, *The Art of Writing*, CUP, 1916, Guild Books, 1946.

11. Morna D Hooker, *The Gospel According to St Mark*, Black's New Testament Commentaries, A & C Black, 1991, p.393.

12. N T Wright, *Twelve Months of Sundays: Reflections on Bible Readings Year A*, SPCK, 2001, p.80.

Chapter 10

1. I owe this poem to Raymond Short.

2. Alastair G Hunter, 'Whose Land Is It Anyway?', in Robert P Carroll and Alastair G Hunter, eds., *Words at Work: Using the Bible in the Academy, the Community and the Churches*, Trinity St Mungo Press, 1994, p.41.

3. Derrick Greeves, 'Harvest 1983', *The Expository Times* 94, 1982-83, 368.

4. John Donne, 'Third Satire':

   On a huge hill,
   Cragged and steep, Truth stands, and he that will
   Reach her, about must, and about must go;
   And what the hill's suddenness resists, win so.

5. Colin Gunton, *Theology Through Preaching*, T & T Clark, 2001, p.67.

6. Michael J Townsend, 'The Use of Poetry in Worship, Preaching and Small Groups', *The Expository Times* 99, 1987-88, 132, reprinted in C S Rodd, ed., *The Pastor's Opportunities*, T & T Clark, 1990, pp.5–6.

Chapter 11

1. Thomas Hardy, *Under the Greenwood Tree*, Penguin Classics, 1985, p.99.

2. *Preacher* in italics represents the invented preacher of dull sermons. His or her sermon is also in italics.

3. John Fenton in Leslie Houlden and John Rogerson, eds., *Common Worship Lectionary: A Scripture Commentary Year A*, SPCK, 2001, p.27–28.

4. George Herbert, 'The Church Porch' stanza 72, in *The Complete English Poems,* Penguin Classics, 1991, p.20.

5. These notes seem to me to be so appalling that I forbear to name the author.

6. I have discussed this more fully in my Epworth Commentary, *The Book of Job,* Epworth Press, 1990, 72-80, pp.120-125.

Chapter 12

1. W F Stuckey tells of the summers he used to spend on the smallholding of his grandfather in Somerset. Towards the end of the holidays the ladders came out and they started picking apples. The apples were packed in a round bushel basket. Every so often his grandfather would put a very special apple to one side. 'That's for Harvest Festival,' he would say. 'Only the very best for God. Remember that, my son!', *The Expository Times*, 98, 1986-87, p.344.